I0800119

Gratitude

Being thankful, appreciating sobriety, helping others and living life to its fullest

AAGRAPEVINE, Inc.

New York, New York

WWW. AAGRAPEVINE.ORG

BOOKS PUBLISHED BY AA GRAPEVINE, INC.

The Language of the Heart (& eBook)
The Best of the Grapevine Volumes I, II, III
The Best of Bill (& eBook)
Thank You for Sharing
Spiritual Awakenings I & II (& eBooks)
I Am Responsible: The Hand of AA
Emotional Sobriety I & II—The Next Frontier (& eBooks)
In Our Own Words: Stories of Young AAs in Recovery (& eBook)
Beginners' Book (& eBook)
Voices of Long-Term Sobriety (& eBook)
A Rabbit Walks Into A Bar
Step by Step—Real AAs, Real Recovery (& eBook)
Young & Sober (& eBook)
Into Action (& eBook)
Happy, Joyous & Free (& eBook)
One on One (& eBook)
No Matter What (& eBook)
Grapevine Daily Quote Book (& eBook)
Sober & Out (& eBook)
Forming True Partnerships (& eBook)
Our Twelve Traditions (& eBook)
Making Amends (& eBook)
Voices of Women in AA (& eBook)
AA in the Military (& eBook)
One Big Tent (& eBook)
Take Me to Your Sponsor (& eBook)
Free on the Inside (& eBook)
Prayer & Meditation (& eBook)
Fun in Sobriety (& eBook)
The Home Group: Heartbeat of AA-30th Anniversary Ed. (& eBook)
Our Twelve Steps (& eBook)

IN SPANISH

El lenguaje del corazón
Lo mejor de Bill (& eBook)
El grupo base: Corazón de AA
Lo mejor de La Viña
Felices, alegres y libres (& eBook)
Un día a la vez (& eBook)
Frente A Frente (& eBook)
Bajo El Mismo Techo (& eBook)
Sobriedad emocional (& eBook)

IN FRENCH

Le langage du coeur
Les meilleurs articles de Bill
Le Groupe d'attache: Le battement du coeur des AA
En tête à tête (& eBook)
Heureux, joyeux et libres (& eBook)
La sobriété émotive

Gratitude

Being thankful, appreciating sobriety, helping others and living life to its fullest

AAGRAPEVINE, Inc.
New York, New York
WWW. AAGRAPEVINE.ORG

475 Riverside Drive
New York, New York 10115

ISBN: Print 978-1-938642-89-0
Printed in Canada

AA Preamble

Alcoholics Anonymous is a fellowship of people
who share their experience, strength and hope with each
other that they may solve their common problem
and help others to recover from alcoholism.

The only requirement for membership is a desire to stop drinking.
There are no dues or fees for AA membership;
we are self-supporting through our own contributions.
AA is not allied with any sect, denomination, politics, organization
or institution; does not wish to engage in any controversy,
neither endorses nor opposes any causes.

Our primary purpose is to stay sober
and help other alcoholics to achieve sobriety.

Contents

AA Preamble . . . . *V*
Welcome . . . . *XI*

CHAPTER ONE

Special Bonds

Reaching out and sharing with one another—the joy of being part of a loving Fellowship

You Made My Day *April 2004* *2*
A Special Bond *February 2025* *4*
Good Things to Come *September 2020* *5*
My Oasis *October 2020* *8*
Soaking in the Sun *September 2024* *10*
The Grateful 5 *December 2020* *13*
Batter Up! *January 2024* *14*

CHAPTER TWO

Family Lost—and Found

Getting to understand, repair, and sometimes rejoin relationships that run far and deep

Time Mended *May 2025* *18*
A Mother's Day Wish *May 2024* *19*
Enjoying the Mess *May 2020* *22*
A Little Boy's Prayer *December 2024* *24*
Sober Sisters *February 2024* *26*
Family Tree *October 2020* *29*
The Reclaimed Turkey Carver *December 1975* *29*

Chapter Three

The Joys of Sponsorship

Loving, trusting and helping each other recover, one on one

I Laughed, He Laughed *May 2020* 32
7 Hours and a Box of Tissues *May 2025* 35
17 Years of Hope *June 2020* 37
3 Guys, 4 Miracles *August 2024* 38
I Want What She Has *June 2025* 40
Team Bob *February 2020* 42
Starting Over *January 2025* 43

Chapter Four

Getting Through Tough Times

Being grateful for a program, the tools and a loving Fellowship to get through adversity

In My Darkest Hour *February 2020* 46
Accepting the Road Ahead *February 2024* 48
Faith & Flashlights *February 2024* 50
A Grateful Holiday *January 2020* 53
So Worth Living *February 2024* 55
Up From the Ashes *September 2020* 57
Acceptance & Gratitude *January 2025* 59
What I Know for Sure *February 2025* 60

Chapter Five

A Place We Can Call Home

Joining a home group, belonging, helping out—a place to recover that you love

Where Attraction Happens *June 2025* 64
Firepit Fanatics *April 2025* 65

Happy to See My Friends *February 2025* 66
Finally Home *April 2020* 68
Letters From Home *July 2024* 70
Best Cake & Coffee Going *May 2020* 71
The Sweet Smell of Coffee *April 2020* 72

CHAPTER SIX

Doing Our Part—Helping Others

One of the great gifts of doing service is what you get back in return

Coffee Queen *May 2020* 76
Maximum Picnic *July 2018* 78
Inside Raymondville *December 2020* 81
It Keeps Getting Better *September 2025* 83
In Service of Service *May 2024* 85
Family Affair *January 2017* 86
Saying Yes *January 2016* 87
Doing My Part *May 2024* 88

CHAPTER SEVEN

Belief & Faith

The joy of finding and connecting with something bigger than us

Whisper of Freedom *October 2020* 92
I Hear the Message *May 2014* 93
Talking to Air *September 2024* 94
Glad to Be Here *September 2025* 97
Heaven on Earth *April 2024* 100
More Than Enough *January 2020* 102
Sweeter and Sweeter *March 2017* 103
A Place in the Sun *February 2016* 103

CHAPTER EIGHT

Living Life to Its Fullest

Enjoying sobriety, getting back into the world, making your dreams come true

Dreams Come True *September 2025* 108
Friends in Every Port *August 2023* 110
Hitting the Road *May 2025* 111
Be Anything, Go Anywhere *August 2023* 113
Joy on a Full Moon *November 2024* 114
Off to the Races *March 2017* 117
The Rowdiest, Rockingest Group *March 2017* 120

CHAPTER NINE

The Gift of Gratitude

Taking time to remember that gratitude is always within reach

A Deep Breath *October 2024* 124
Another Beautiful Year *January 2025* 125
One of Those Days *February 2024* 126
The Gift of Gratitude *November 2024* 127
Going in the Right Direction *September 2025* 129
Etched in Stone *May 2024* 130
Trying to Be Ungrateful *March 2020* 131

Twelve Steps 134
Twelve Traditions 135
About AA and AA Grapevine 136

Welcome

The inspiring personal stories in this book—all of which appeared in Grapevine—express gratitude in its many manifestations, illustrating how it's one of the great gifts of sobriety.

Sometimes Grapevine readers are simply grateful for the beauty of life itself, as seen in the story "Sober Sisters," by Susan and Lynda C., where Lynda writes about the happiness she feels "gazing at a sunset, listening to the rain, walking, reading, learning, enjoying silences." Or gratitude can arrive after seemingly small events, as in the story "Finally Home," when L.M., a member who has relapsed repeatedly, is entrusted with signing the lease of their home group's meeting space.

Gratitude can also be a revelation that helps us through painful moments. While describing her difficult divorce in her story "A Deep Breath," Stefania R. tells us, "Gratitude is a state of mind, an emotion, an attitude, a condition of the soul, a prayer (if you will.) ... If I stay in an attitude of gratitude, I can pretty much deal with anything."

True thankfulness may have been difficult for many of us to feel during our drinking days, preoccupied as we were with where our next drink (or resentment) was coming from. This is what makes gratitude in sobriety so precious to us now. Plus, feeling grateful actually feels good! We may feel gratitude after a casual coffee with friends, making amends to an elderly family member, or watching our children grow into wonderful adults knowing they have never seen us drunk.

AA's cofounder Bill W. once wrote, "Gratitude should go forward, rather than backward ... if you carry the message to still others, you will be making the best possible repayment for the help given you." The writers of the stories in *Gratitude*, AA members of all ages, lengths of sobriety and backgrounds, know that to be alive and sober is to be grateful.

CHAPTER ONE

Special Bonds

Reaching out and sharing with one another—the joy of being part of a loving Fellowship

What many of us remember most from our first AA meetings are the people who greet us at the door, buy us a Big Book or hand us a warm cup of coffee. It's the beginning of a fellowship, which is this chapter's focus. However, affection isn't always immediate. In his story "A Special Bond," Gary C.—now celebrating nearly 50 years of sobriety—writes, "These people were nothing like me and I wanted nothing to do with them." Today Gary has lunch every few months with "these people." Each one of these guys, he writes, "has something I want."

The stories in this chapter movingly capture the intense, sometimes lifelong bonds of gratitude and love formed in diners, homes, softball diamonds, prisons or even during epic blizzards. The well-traveled Brian S., in his story "Good Things to Come," describes international travels during which he attends meetings where members speak Finnish, Hindi and Spanish, none of which he understands. But that doesn't matter. He's grateful because they have one common purpose—speaking the language of the heart.

You Made My Day

April 2004

The Arizona sun had chased away all but a few clouds. Chirping birds tattled on a couple of the ducks who squabbled, seemingly about nothing. From their rocky sunbathing hangout, one of the turtles swam across the sky blue water to check out my standup paddleboard. I could have stayed there forever. I relished the wonders of this day and thanked God for sobriety, the paddle and Tucson life.

As I left the lake reluctantly and packed up, I said a prayer for all the alcoholics I knew personally who had "life stuff" happening, such as new sobriety, and family or medical issues. Then I added, "Please God, help those inside and outside the rooms who are still suffering and their families." Odd that I added that part that day—it was not something I always thought to add.

Everything was loaded up in the car. I was about to start the engine when I recognized the laid-back, outdoorsy dude with a huge smile and a kayak on his car. As he walked up, he thanked me for a lead I had given him one day on another lake to check out, a lake I hadn't even been to yet myself, by the way. It turns out he and his fiancee had been there twice since I recommended it, and they loved it. Then he mentioned it was his birthday, and I sang Happy Birthday to him. It always makes people smile even though I sound terrible doing it.

I asked him if he was going to kayak, and he said he was going to fish first. He was waiting for his fiancee to show up. I asked what else he was going to do for his birthday. Was he going to dinner?

"Yes," he replied. Then he said out of nowhere, "I haven't had a drink in a few years, and I really want to drink a ton of vodka to remember how bad it makes me feel hungover and terrible!" He went on to say that he used to drink a liter of vodka a day. I asked him if he knew what a friend of Bill W. was. He didn't, and I said it's someone in Alcoholics Anonymous and that I was a recovering alcoholic.

He said he was too and had tried AA for a while. I told him that if I started drinking again, I knew I wouldn't be able to stop. He shook his head and agreed he probably couldn't either. I smiled and told him, "God was definitely at work here." I asked, "What are the chances of you coming up to me and talking about this? How about you drink vodka tomorrow?" I suggested.

"Yeah, that sounds good," he responded. "I'll drink it tomorrow, not today." We left each other with a knowing smile and a "See you soon."

Driving away, I was at peace. With a deep sigh, I thought of why I continue to go to meetings. One reason is to remember that alcohol is cunning, baffling and powerful, and I just don't need to drink today, no matter what. I said a prayer for the dude at the lake and thanked God for meeting him. Life is good sober!

I thought I wouldn't see him again, but a few days later I was back at the lake paddling, a healthier obsession. Just as I was about to make my turn, I heard someone in a loud voice say, "I didn't drink the other day, thanks to you!" It was the birthday dude. I yelled back, "I prayed for you the entire day, and today you just made mine by telling me that news." A big smile spread over his face. "You certainly made mine the other day," he said.

By the grace of God and sharing the AA message, the dude at the lake and I had another day sober and that's how it works, a day at a time.

Cori C.
Tucson, Arizona

A Special Bond

February 2025

I went to lunch yesterday with three close AA friends at a trendy restaurant in Denver that was voted as having one of the best Philly steak sandwiches in town. The guys ranged in age from 64 to 94. We get together like this every few months and, when we're lucky, we're accompanied by a woman friend in the program who happens to be from my home state of Minnesota. But this day it was just the guys.

Our lunch was not that different from many previous ones. We enjoyed lots of laughter and stories from the past, traded stories of what our grown kids are up to and discussed current events. However, this particular lunch had a deep and profound impact on me.

I went to my first AA meeting in November 1976. I was 20 years old at the time and the meeting was for young people at a sober clubhouse in Minneapolis. People there were laughing, joking around, hugging, and at the end they all held hands and closed with a prayer. These people were nothing like me and I wanted nothing to do with them. AA was not for me, I was sure.

I managed to stay sober for 10 days straight, a record I had not achieved in several years. I don't remember how or why I started drinking again. I just remember the deep, dark cliff my life went down over the next couple of months. After an arrest (my fourth) in January of 1977, I found a little humility, or humiliation, and sought help. I went back to AA and have not had a drink since. I found out "those people" were just like me and they would be central to my recovery.

OK, let's go back to our lunch yesterday. It dawned on me as we left that all four of us hugged each other in the middle of a very busy restaurant. I didn't give it a second thought at the time, but what a shift this was from how I thought back in 1976. It made me grateful to reflect on how much AA had changed me over the last 46 years. I also thought about how much more I want to change. Each one of these guys has something I want.

It happened to be Presidents' Day that day, so I asked which president they respected the most. Our 94-year-old friend told us his favorite, based on the positive messages he had always communicated during his presidency. There was no talk of politics at our table. This inspired me to focus more on the good things instead of our differences.

Another fellow inspires me with his tireless dedication to others and how he is taking action every day related to his AA service positions. The third friend, a fellow Minnesotan, started playing hockey when he turned 50. He's now 64 and still plays a pickup game on a regular basis. I admire his zest for life.

I appreciate my friends. Each of them contributes to life and inspires others. They certainly inspire me. I'm so grateful for them. Together we have learned to give hugs and to be hugged, no matter where we are.

Gary C.
Arvada, Colorado

Good Things to Come

September 2020

Her letter was annoying and intrusive. How dare she? I hadn't seen my older sister in, well, I didn't know how long it had been. Her letter stated that my drinking was out of control and I needed to get help.

I was a solitary drinker. That is, until I would go into a blackout and leave my apartment to wander the streets of the dying, formerly industrial town where I lived. Occasionally, I would find mementos of my blackout travels—a snow shovel in the hallway, a book on my table—with no recollection of where they had come from.

I learned later that what precipitated my sister's sharp missive were the phone calls I made to my parents during my blackouts.

Four months after my 22nd birthday, I made a half-hearted call for help. I had never heard of AA, but I found a number for an "Alcoholism Hotline" in the phonebook. It was a toll-free call, so I dialed the number at 7:45 in the morning. I assumed no one would answer at that hour and then I could be satisfied that I had tried to get help for my round-the-clock drinking. Instead, a woman named Rosemary answered. She asked me if I had a problem with drinking. I said I did. She said, "So did I. I'm an alcoholic."

My next thought was, Then what the hell am I talking to you for? But then something unexpected happened. A felt a surge of relief at Rosemary's words. The huge burden of shame I felt at being unable to control my drinking tumbled away.

Two days later, I got a phone call from a man named Mike. We arranged that he would pick me up for an AA meeting the next day. It was a Friday and 18 inches of snow had just fallen. Mike called me on Friday afternoon to confirm.

"There's still a meeting?" I asked, hoping for a reprieve. "There's a lot of snow out there and the roads don't look good."

"Did you have any trouble getting something to drink today?" Mike replied. The answer of course was no. When Mike came by to pick me up he had a slab of granite in the bed of his pickup truck to weigh it down in the snow. Off we went to the meeting. About 30 people were inside, including three speakers who had come all the way from another town. Though I did identify with a woman who told a story of trying with toothbrush and paste to scrub the alcohol smell out of her breath before work (something I had tried), I was not ready to jump into this AA thing with both feet.

My brilliant idea instead was to implement a marijuana-maintenance program. After all, my problem was with alcohol, not marijuana. I had a calendar with a box for each day. One slash meant I drank no alcohol that day. A second slash meant I used neither alcohol nor pot. There would be three days of one slash followed by three days with two. Marijuana always led me back to my drug of choice—liquor.

There's a saying in our program—bring the body and the mind will follow. Mike and his buddies loaded me in the back of their cars and took me to meetings despite my reservations. One day I even passed out in an AA meeting in a treatment center at which they were speaking. When it was over, they just roused me and took me home.

Mike didn't give up on me though. I only did one right thing during those first months—I kept going to meetings. And I rarely spoke, which was a remarkable and uncharacteristic exhibition of good sense, as I had not much of value to share.

Then something happened. On May 4, 1978, my calendar had one slash—no alcohol consumed that day. The next day was warm and sunny with the earthy scent of spring in the air. My drug dealer peddled up to me on his bike in front of my apartment and offered to share a joint with me—for free no less. I was standing there with my girlfriend. Something else, a Higher Power, was also present with the three of us. All of a sudden, the words, "No, thanks," tumbled out of my mouth. My girlfriend's jaw dropped. She was visibly shocked.

That turned out to be my first day of sobriety. Shortly thereafter, I threw the calendar away. Later I would come to understand that I had learned two things in those first three months of slipping and sliding. The first was that I had brought my body and my mind did follow. The second was that I can't think myself into right action, but I can act myself into right thinking. Going to meetings was the right action.

The best thing about finding AA when I did was that I could be sober not only for the good things to come in my 20s, but also especially for the sad things.

Less than three years after that spring day, my younger brother was diagnosed with cancer and I became his bone marrow donor. My sadness at his eventual death was tempered with gratitude. I was present for his death. I did what I needed to do and got to say goodbye to him before he died because I was sober.

That first decade in AA I earned a college degree and married that remarkable young woman who had been standing next to me when I said, "No, thanks." I also witnessed the birth of our three daughters and fell into a great career.

It's been 42 years since that first wintry meeting with Mike and I'm still very much a meeting maker. As I've heard, "people who don't go to meetings don't find out what happens to people who don't go to meetings." I've learned that the only things you need to start a new meeting are a resentment and a coffeepot, and I've done that twice.

I frequently travel internationally for my job and I always center my trip around an AA meeting (or two, if I can find them). In a four-week period earlier this year, I attended meetings on four continents. I've attended meetings in many languages, including Finnish, Hindi and Spanish, none of which I speak. I go because I just need to be with people who speak our language of the heart.

I've received many gifts in AA, including a connection with a Higher Power, reconciliation with my family and the creation of a new one. Perhaps the greatest gift I've received is a love affair with meetings and our stories—and those make everything else possible. I can also have a meeting with myself, even when two or more of us have not physically gathered. You're holding it in your hand.

Brian S.
Wyckoff, New Jersey

My Oasis

October 2020

Bob Dylan sang about being a rolling stone, and I was one too. I've moved a lot in my life. My father was transferred just about every four years when I was growing up.

By the time I left home, moving was "in my blood." So when my restlessness during my drinking days arose when a living situation became intolerable, I would simply move somewhere else a few miles away.

I have lived in the Seattle area for 35 years. I was always looking for "greener pastures" and really never found them. Of course, I was drinking and moving and changing jobs too. Mostly, I was just plain miserable. This slowly changed in sobriety.

When I was 12 years sober, my father died. I lost my job the week after his funeral. He and my mother had been "snow birds" for 17 years and finally settled in Tucson, Arizona. With nothing to keep me in Seattle, down I went! I had been dreading the move, so a friend went with me to comfort me as we headed south.

I finally reached my new home on the west side of the Tucson Mountains. There was a desert gully out back, so I had a front row seat for the entire cycle of the seasons in the Sonoran Desert. I took care of my elderly mother, while I worked full-time. I had to sell two houses, two vehicles and a trailer. I had to downsize their accumulated belongings.

I found a meeting place close to home. It was a mile away from the base of Cat Mountain. The first time I went, I found it was like many of the AA meetings I had gone to before. But soon something unusual happened. The leader started with, "My name is Charlie, I am an alcoholic and I'm a member of the such-and-such group." That was familiar. But then the members all chimed in, saying, "Right on!" in unison. You have got to be kidding me, I thought. This was not a response I had heard before. I knew that meetings are autonomous, but this was just a little hokey, in my opinion.

Nonetheless, I kept coming back each week. This AA group, composed mainly of men, became my sole support for the three years I lived there. Before I knew it, I was chiming in just like everyone else.

The meetings there began with "How It Works." The Traditions were read out of a Second edition Big Book and then the group decided what the topic would be that evening. When no one suggested a topic, Charlie would blurt out, "Gratitude." And so it went on, just like that. Each group member took a turn doing the setup and leading the meeting.

During the rainy summer season, we met outside. Cat Mountain was not too far away so we had wildlife to accompany us, including lizards and crickets, as well as the occasional snake, tarantula and black widow. Millipedes, centipedes and scorpions were always at hand.

The members of the meeting were an unlikely bunch of drunks. There was a fireman from Cape Cod, a guy with a beard more than a foot long who brought his chihuahua, a fellow who got sober in prison, a coworker of mine who I could talk to about the pressures of my responsibilities, a guy who sold tools and a married couple who had a young daughter. We were a very tight-knit group, and when the wife of one of our members left him, the group rallied around. We were there later when he got the news that she had collapsed and died in a convenience store at age 38 from alcoholism.

This meeting was my oasis in the desert and kept me sober for three years. I'm truly grateful for this little meeting. We carried the message out in the middle of nowhere, out there for people like me who needed to be somewhere safe and surrounded by sobriety—centipedes and all.

Marcy B.
Bothell, Washington

Soaking in the Sun

September 2024

I was approached by a friend from my home group a while back about writing an article on getting sober young. He said he wanted to know what could possibly have compelled me to want to get sober at such an early age. So, here's my story.

When I first got to AA I can't say that getting sober was something I wanted. I was 24 and I felt half out of my mind. I was suffering from one panic attack after another, and I could barely see straight. I wasn't going to meetings. I didn't have a sponsor and I'd had two recent relapses. After 30 days of being dry, more than anything I wanted to get out of my own skin.

But the seed of sobriety that had been planted by my previous two attempts to stop drinking finally began to take root. I was desperate.

I picked up the phone and called a woman who had told her story in a meeting the first night I walked into AA. I asked her for help. She very gently guided me into a program of rigorous action that brought me into a life well beyond my wildest dreams.

My first home group was a large meeting. It was an eclectic group, you might say. I felt more strongly that I belonged there than I had ever felt anywhere in my life. Although I had friends of all ages, all backgrounds and all walks of life, if not for this fellowship of young people within that home group, I'm not sure I would have kept coming back.

Having a group of young people my age allowed me to experience the excitement of being in my 20s without having to drink. We traveled everywhere together, to AA conventions and roundups. We sat on rooftops of beach houses soaking up the sun and staring out into the ocean. We sat in the back of diners smoking cigarettes until two in the morning, talking about everything under the sun. We dressed "to the nines" for alkathons and danced like no one was watching. We went to our favorite concerts and danced at clubs. We laughed together, cried together and celebrated together.

One of my favorite memories was the time I faced a true hardship in my sobriety. I had recently lost both a job and a relationship. I got to see how God shows up in my life. That day I was dragged to a meeting by my roommate. After the much-needed meeting was over, a few of my young sober friends came and asked me to go hang out with them downtown. I cried on about how I lost my job and needed to figure that out. "Great, you don't have to get up for work in the morning, so you can go with us!," one of them said. "But I don't have my keys or my cell phone," I replied. "Why do you need your keys and cell phone?" they asked. I looked at them and shrugged. "Well, I guess I don't," I said.

With that, I let go and jumped into the car with my fellows and headed downtown without any expectations or reservations. We played in the water fountain. We ate ice cream. We danced in the streets with the street musician. Then we came back to the parking lot of a local grocery store at four in the morning and played soccer in the empty parking lot. That was by far one of the best nights of my life. God and my fellows showed up!

Over the years, we have watched each other grow up in the rooms. A lot of us are still here. Some of us got to make it through college and start careers. We bought our first cars or even our first houses. A lot of us got married and had children. We also suffered loss and heartache. But we continued to stay sober and to stay committed to our primary purpose through whatever life had dealt us.

When I came in at 24, I was convinced that I had drunk my entire life away. I thought my life was beyond repair and I was doomed to loneliness and despair. Today I'm 44. Last year I celebrated 20 years sober. I've been sober now longer than I drank. I also celebrated 10 years of marriage to a man who has never seen me drunk. He sees me as the woman I wanted to become. My husband and I have two absolutely beautiful young children who have also never seen me drink and, God willing, they never will. Who knew at 24 that my life was actually just beginning?

I do not take this disease lightly. It's constantly progressing, so my program of recovery must also be in a state of progression. Today I stay active in my Steps, work with sponsees, go to about four meetings a week and do service.

I realize I am now one of the old people the young newcomers see when they walk in the rooms for the first time. So I make it a point to always reach out and reassure them that I was once where they are now and I get it. I support young people's conventions and groups to attract newcomers to a new way of life, so they too don't have to drink away their lives and come in much later than they have to. That was the gift that was so generously given to me.

Anonymous
Summerville, South Carolina

The Grateful 5

December 2020

I am an alcoholic in recovery in a prison in Northeast Florida. I'm doing time as a direct result of my alcoholism. I had about a year of sobriety before I had to start my prison sentence. I have been actively involved in AA in prison and I've done anything I can to help other men who want to change.

I was very excited to find out upon arriving at my current facility that there was a Monday night Step Workshop that was inmate-led, a Tuesday afternoon Big Book meeting led by an outside volunteer, and a Thursday night, rather large open discussion meeting also led by an outside AA volunteer. Pretty good for prison recovery.

But when COVID struck, our meetings in here stopped, just like you guys out there. The prison stopped the outside volunteers and all the meetings.

AAs on the outside are fortunate enough to have the internet to meet. We inmates aren't so lucky, so we had to try to find another way. Unfortunately, we are quarantined by dorm, so getting together on the rec yard was not an option. I encouraged the guys to try to meet in their dorm and I even snuck my issues of Grapevine over to them. That made me happy.

Despite many obstacles, our Higher Power has made a way for us to adapt and overcome. I'm in a dorm of about 200 men. A few of us guys decided we'd try to make our own AA meeting in a tiny nearby cell, and that's exactly what we've done. Every Wednesday night at 7 P.M., the five of us mask up, grab our Big Books and coffee cups and we meet. No computer meeting for us, just an awesome face-to-face AA meeting. Amazingly, the five of us have truly opened up with each other and built the kind of trust that's often difficult to find in a prison setting.

Most important? All five of us have remained sober throughout this stressful period. We are truly grateful.

Wes A.
Lawtey, Florida

Batter Up!

January 2024

I came into AA one December day. By spring, I was familiar enough with my home group to understand the announcements at the beginning of meetings. And there was one announcement I definitely paid attention to: "Our group's softball team will hold practice in the park this Sunday afternoon."

I knew the park and had the day off that Sunday (because it was Sunday and also because I was unemployed!), yet I refused to show up. Playing softball suddenly didn't seem like an option for me. I was a newcomer and an introvert who didn't exactly want to be noticed or seen in meetings. Luckily, I had a sponsor by then and I kept showing up to meetings with her.

Fast forward to the next spring. Announcements for sober softball practice started back up again. This time I had more sober time and knew a few more people in the program, but I was still too uncomfortable in my own skin to join everyone on the field. I showed up to a game early in the summer, mostly to find my sponsor and talk to her as we watched them play. The team was one player short that game, but when I was asked if I could join, I refused. I had intentionally worn the wrong shoes to ensure I couldn't play.

Later in the season, my friend in the program started playing on our group's softball team and I showed up to a game to cheer her on. It was a special double-header. My AA group had the city's Parks Department turn the field lights on to illuminate the field on a hot summer night. I knew many members from our home group who came to watch, and I enjoyed talking with members in the stands late into the night.

As the days got shorter and the softball season wrapped up, I finally decided to play at one of the last games of the year. I made sure to go to a meeting beforehand and to wear the right shoes. When I got to the game, I realized I knew almost everyone on the team. Since I had no equipment, a member lent me their glove and asked if I could be the catcher. As a lone wolf, I hadn't played a team sport in decades, but it was wonderful to feel the ball in my glove as I caught each pitch and used my arm to catapult it back to the pitcher.

When it was my turn to bat, I noticed how calm I was in the batter's box. The nervousness I had felt as a newcomer amazingly had been replaced by serenity. The first pitch was lobbed toward home plate and I figured, why not swing since this seems like a good one. Wow, base hit! I got on first and my friend was on second. We were both driven home by the next batter, a newcomer I'd never met before that night but felt compelled to give an exuberant high five to in the dugout.

After the game, I was struck by the spiritual growth I had to undergo to have fun that night. The guide for living offered by AA is what transformed me from a fearful newcomer to a relaxed member of the Fellowship and for that, I'm so grateful. Time to play ball!

Jenna W.
Kansas, Missouri

CHAPTER TWO

Family Lost—and Found

Getting to understand, repair, and sometimes rejoin relationships that run far and deep

Chapter two deals with the positive changes sobriety can bring to many families. In our AA literature, Bill W. writes about the inability of active alcoholics "to form a true partnership with another human being." Yet, on the flip side of that, sobriety can bring much hope. Many alcoholics, once separated from their loved ones, can experience love and gratitude when they begin to repair relationships with family members.

But it's often not easy, as Mary Ann G. attests in her story "A Mother's Day Wish." Having given up her son for adoption, she "stumbled into rehab angry, hungover and dazed," and sobered up. It took time, but she reconnected with her son and experienced the gratitude that only someone who feels they have a lost a child forever can feel.

Whether it's a sober grandfather discovering his love for his grandson, even as the toddler tears up toilet paper rolls, or a sober dad finally allowed to reclaim his Thanksgiving turkey-carving duties, gratitude for the renewal of family is sweet reward for having found one's way to sobriety.

Time Mended

May 2025

I was born the second of three sons. We were 10, 7 and 6 years old when my parents split up. Mom and us boys moved into a three-bedroom apartment with my maternal grandparents. My father disappeared and never sent any alimony or child-support payments. I was embarrassed because my parents were divorced and because I didn't have a father in my life. Also, we didn't live in a single-family home like my friends did.

I didn't get along with my crusty, less-than-affectionate grandfather. He was a veteran of World War I and told us that he had been in Germany when the Armistice was signed. To celebrate the end of the war, he bought a pocket watch and had it engraved with his initials. With the arrogance of youth and the mid-teen onset of my alcoholism, I treated him shabbily because I saw him as cranky, old and uneducated, while I saw myself as young and cool.

Actually, my grandfather generously extended himself to my mother and my brothers and me. He took us in when he didn't have to, all while helping my grandmother recover from a stroke. She died soon after we moved in. At that time, my grandfather was on the eve of retirement, and he didn't charge my mother any rent. He also made lunch for me and my brothers every day and invented chores for us to do so he could give us an allowance. Due to my self-centered world view, all of this was lost on me at the time.

During my first visit back to my hometown after joining AA, I met with my grandfather to make amends for the disrespectful way I had treated him over the years. There were some difficult things I needed to share with him, and he listened patiently.

When I was done, he said the words every young man yearns to hear from his father, for this is what he was to me: "Well, I think you're going to be OK now." Then he gave me his engraved pocket watch from the war. He didn't give it to either of his two sons, who were both World War II veterans, nor to any of his other many grandchildren. He gave it to me, the skinny, obnoxious kid who hectored him mercilessly for years and then tried to make it right.

Our relationship blossomed after that day, largely because I treated him with dignity and respect, which all of us deserve. Our interactions became easier. I visited my grandfather regularly. I listened attentively to tales of his youth. We joked around often.

My wife and I picked his birthday for our wedding day. When he entered a VA nursing home, we visited him there. He asked me to be a pallbearer when he died, and I was honored to do so. The spirit and essence of the Ninth Step is about improving relationships and that's what happened when I treated my grandfather with the dignity and respect he deserved.

Some years ago, I entered that stage of life where I'm giving away family heirlooms. My son has that pocket watch now and we didn't need to make amends to each other in order for me to give it to him, because thanks to AA, we already treat each other with dignity and respect.

Paul C.
Oceanside, California

A Mother's Day Wish

May 2024

Two years before I got to AA, I gave birth to a baby boy. He was beautiful and healthy, but I was not so beautiful or ready to take on the responsibility of raising a child. I gave him away. Before leaving the hospital, I had the nurse unwrap my son from his blanket so I could see his fingers and toes. I just knew I couldn't hold him because I would never let him go. I left the hospital without a tear. I held it in to not show my parents or others how broken my heart was. Instead, I buried my feelings in alcohol.

I can't remember most of the next two years, as I drank to black out or pass out. I often thought of suicide. The EAP director at my steel company would tell me, "Mary Ann, you are an alcoholic. If you stop drinking you will get better. You will." So in 1982, after living a life of sex, drugs and rock and roll, I stumbled into rehab angry, hungover and dazed to save my job. I was 22 years old.

After I got sober, the guilt of giving up my son was first and foremost in my mind. On my first sober Mother's Day I went to my AA meeting, hoping to distract my thoughts. While walking to my car after the meeting, a woman walking in the same direction turned and asked if I had children. I answered, "Yes, a son, but I don't have him." She responded that she had two but didn't have them either. We looked at each other and kept walking. I learned that morning that when I think I have it bad, someone else always has it worse.

When I got my two years, I had my first miracle of sobriety. My daughter was born. I had her in the same hospital and same room where I had my son. This time I was ready to be a sober mom. A year later my next miracle happened. My second daughter was born at Christmas. These days were some of the happiest times in my life. But all the while, in the back of my mind, I would wonder where and how my son was.

I called the place that had information about my son for years, but got nowhere. I finally had to surrender. I turned him over and trusted he was in good hands. Knowing he was a chosen child helped to ease my heartache. I knew that his parents had waited three years for a baby. I kept my profile at the organization updated just in case he might one day seek me out.

Many years later, in 2019, my daughter was watching a TV show about finding people. She asked me about her brother and suggested I try once more, so I did. A new woman worked in the adoption department, and she had an empathic ear. After doing a search on her computer, she told me that my son was very findable. I felt like God touched my life once again.

I filled out an application. I was ready to face whatever the outcome was to be. Next, I wrote a short introduction letter to see if we were on the same page. He was! We were encouraged to send a few more letters to get to know each other and our purpose for meeting. I longed to know if he was doing well in life. I wanted him to know my door was open and that he was loved. I found myself writing phrases like "more will be revealed" and other AA terms in my letters. Soon the time came when we could talk. He told me he had no resentments about my decision to let him go. He had great parents and a good upbringing. I was so relieved! As he spoke, I noticed that the tone of the words he used was similar to mine—AA like. I was so curious. I asked, "Are you a friend of Bill's?" Turns out he knew exactly what I meant. "Yes!" he said. He had nine years sober, a sponsor and a wonderful network on the other side of town. He had even been to the same H & I commitment I had, but when my cochair was there. The apple doesn't fall far from the tree!

One Monday night, sometime later, I went to a meeting with my dear AA friends Mike and Brenda. I don't usually attend that meeting. I went in and looked around the room. Suddenly I got a wave from a man with a mask (it was during COVID). I knew immediately it was my son! My heart skipped a beat. I was so full of joy, but nervous. He had never been to that meeting either. His sponsor was speaking. I sat there listening. I knew his sponsor from years of service work in AA.

After his sponsor spoke, he called on my son to share. Then he called on me. Then he called on the group of men he brought. After the meeting, I walked over to my son and asked if we could pray together when the meeting closed. We did and then he gave me a big hug. His sponsor came over and my son introduced me as his mom. I couldn't believe what I was hearing after all these years.

Turns out my son's a good man. It was totally in God's time that we would meet. I introduced him to my friend Mike, and Mike picked my son up with a big bear hug and cried. I then introduced him to Brenda, and she cried too. My son told me he felt like a celebrity that night!

Soon after, my son got to meet his sisters and nephews—family full circle. All I ever wanted in life was to be happy and have a family.

My son and I got to share our AA anniversaries. I've been able to pass on my past sobriety chips to him. I heard through the meeting grapevine that my son shared the story of our meeting in one of his other AA meetings. He said he felt it needed to be shared to help others. What a blessing AA is.

I now have more than 40 years sober. I'm truly joyous and free. I've come a long way from that first Mother's Day in AA. But I keep coming back, as miracles never cease in recovery.

Mary Ann G.
Dundalk, Maryland

Enjoying the Mess

May 2020

It was time to take my grandson home after spending a day together. It was around 9:00 in the evening. He had had his bath and was in his pajamas, but he was stalling. I could hear his priceless giggles in the other room. I was clueless about what he was doing but he sounded so happy. I stood at the door listening to him and my memories of the past slid in.

Was there any laughter like this when I was out drinking? No, mostly tears. I was moaning in pain and self-pity. But laughter? Never.

My drinking history is familiar to most alcoholics. I was a hot mess. I had been arrested for my third DUI. I had crossed that invisible line from social drinking into daily need. I was defeated by alcohol. It owned me totally. I could not make any decisions. My life consisted of quickly finishing what I had to do so I could start drinking to ease my pain.

I was middle-aged with two failed marriages behind me. I had lost a child in a car accident. The driver who killed my child was over the legal limit of alcohol and was looking at significant time in prison. And yet, there I was turning into the very thing that killed my child.

But now I'm sober and I'm spending time with my 5-year-old

grandson. His laughter is infectious. I called out to him to say it was time to leave and yet he continued to laugh. When he finally came to the kitchen and sat on my lap, he had a mischievous look in his eye. I told him how much I loved him, put his coat on and placed him in his booster seat to drive him home.

When I dropped him off and returned home, I looked in the bathroom. He had unrolled the entire roll of toilet paper. It was heaped on the floor in so many directions. The pile of paper was just like my life had been when I drank. There was no way to see where anything started and where it ended. As I looked at this pile of endless paper, I began laughing so hard. I dropped to my knees and thanked God that I found a better life.

Each day, I'm given a clean slate to write a new day's activity. I can choose. I can use this slate to engage in old behaviors of drinking and self-pity or I can use this clean slate to continue to allow God to give me guidance and inspiration.

Through AA, I am learning how to make and keep personal relationships, the kind I could only imagine when I was drinking. The wonderful and caring souls I meet in AA want nothing from me. We depend on each other. Maybe someone's going through a tough time. A drink may be looking good, or maybe they've had a terrible day. We sober alcoholics have bad days sometimes. We are like others except we just can't drink. It is that easy or hard. The Steps are in order for a purpose. We can't skip around and do the Steps that seem the easiest. It's because of the hard work in AA that I've been given the privilege of having my grandson come to my house.

Some days are better than others. I get sad, I worry, and I experience stress. But I turn these over to God and pray. My grandson keeps me on my toes and I learn something new each day. He's surrounded genetically on both sides by the disease of alcoholism, but I cannot worry; we will cross that road when it's time.

Until then, I will enjoy the show. The toilet paper heaped on the floor reminds me that I never want to return to that old life of pain and tears. I want to be here as long as possible to enjoy the next chapter of my life. I'm grateful that God has a rich sense of humor. I want to laugh so hard that tears roll down my face every day.

M.B.
Marion, Ohio

A Little Boy's Prayer

December 2024

At the end of my drinking, my son was 9 years old and completely frustrated with his father's drinking. I wasn't really sure what he thought of my drinking because we had never discussed it. His father and I had been divorced for years at that time.

I didn't know what to do or say to help my son, so I called my sister Gwen who had been sober for six years in AA. She suggested Al-Anon for him. I took him to Al-Anon, where he got a sponsor and started working the Steps and soon he was able to work out a relationship with his dad.

A few months later he announced to me that he was moving in with his dad and perhaps I could ask his Auntie Gwen for help. I wondered how he knew I needed help and how he knew about my drinking? It was like I was stabbed in my back when he left. That dagger of truth hurt really bad, and my drinking increased suddenly.

For the next few months, my son was very aloof with me as I descended into a hellish life of work, drink, pass out, work, drink, pass out. I got to the point where I couldn't live with alcohol and couldn't live without it.

About nine months after my son moved in with his dad, I just couldn't take it any longer and went to a very dark place. I was in such great pain, and I didn't think I could go on.

One lonely night I picked up the phone and called my sister. She suggested I visit her in Florida and if I didn't like it there, I could return to New Mexico. Thinking that it might be a good idea, I got rid of everything I owned that did not fit in my car and headed off to

Florida. I drove this old car with 97,000 miles on it and bald tires. I had $200 in my pocket.

At this point, I had not connected my pain to my drinking. I didn't even have a clue that alcohol was a problem. I had not indicated any such thing to my sister either. I really felt that if people would just behave, my life would be really good.

Once I got to Florida and arrived at Gwen's house, we talked a while and caught up on some old times. I mentioned my horrible life and how I was a victim of everyone else's bad behavior. After a while she said, "I don't know what's wrong with you, but I'm going to an AA meeting." I told her I would love to go but was afraid they would ask me to quit drinking.

Luckily, eventually I decided to go with her, and much to my surprise I received the most precious and powerful gift there—hope.

I listened to the people there as they shared about their drinking problems and their solutions. At some point during that first meeting, it just came to me: I too must have this. If they can stay sober, maybe I can too. I picked up a white chip at the end of that meeting and, by the grace of God and AA, I have not picked up a drink since. That day was June 27, 1985.

Some time later when my son and I were reunited, he shared love and approval of me and my newfound sobriety. I told him how amazingly different my life is now without alcohol. I told him I admired him for leaving me to go live with his dad. I later came to understand the old-soul wisdom of this little boy who loved me enough to leave me. That was an extremely brave and very loving thing he did for his mother. When I asked him about that difficult choice he made at such a young age, he simply replied, "Mom, I just prayed for a better life for you."

To this day, those words ring through my head. I often ponder in my morning meditation about my sobriety. I know today that God answers prayers. And sometimes I can't help but wonder whether my life is just the answer to a little boy's prayer.

Maddy L.
Placitas, New Mexico

Sober Sisters

February 2024

They say alcoholism is a family disease. Well, my sister and I can sure second that. And the family thread doesn't start or stop with us either, as you will see. Here are our stories, two sisters, both longtime AA members, with sober branches from and to other family members as well.

Let's start with my sister, Susan C. of Maui, Hawaii. Here's her story ...

How exactly does someone stay sober for 32 years? One day at a time is what my mother used to say. She would be considered an oldtimer, as she came into the rooms in the 1960s. I was old enough to go to Alateen, which gave me enough knowledge to know where to go once my alcoholism brought me to my bottom.

Living the program one day at a time has been a key to helping me stay sober and live life. I break things into small pieces. When I was sobering up, I just tried to not drink between meetings. From the morning meeting to the noon meeting to the evening meeting and then again till the next morning, this helped me to get through my first 30, 60 and 90 days.

I didn't start drinking at a young age, maybe because my mother sobered up when I was about 11 and there just wasn't any alcohol around. Once I started going out to clubs with my friends we'd do shots, and then I was off and running.

Even though I knew where to go when I realized that my drinking was not normal, it didn't mean that I knew what to do. I would come into the AA meeting late and leave early. I would shrink down in my chair so no one could see me or call on me. Needless to say, I didn't stay sober.

When I finally surrendered and admitted I was powerless over alcohol and came back into the rooms, I would hear people say, "You only have to stay sober for today. Just do it, as the slogan says, one day at a time."

I thought, Yeah, right, I can't drink for the rest of my life? That means my life is over and I'll never have any fun again. But by staying sober a day at a time, I met others who were new like me. We started hanging out together and supported each other. I had been so closed off from the world because my whole life was centered on drinking that I didn't realize that I wasn't having fun, I was just existing. I blossomed and saw things I never knew existed all around me.

Now I use this slogan, A Day at a Time, to help me get through difficult days and situations. Life doesn't stop providing challenges just because we sober up. I lost jobs and worse, I lost people I loved. If I break life down into smaller pieces, it's a lot easier to handle. Often that means I pray and ask my Higher Power for guidance and then I do the next right thing, as they say, or what's in front of me to do. And by focusing just on today, I've found that I can stay sober and get through anything.

And now me, Lynda C. of New York City: Like Susan, I too thought that stopping drinking meant I wouldn't have fun anymore. In fact, that was one of the last things I said to someone who was trying to Twelfth Step me on the phone the day of my last drink, back in September of 1981. "But drinking is the only fun I have in my life," I said, to which he replied, "Well, it doesn't sound like you're having so much fun now."

It was true. I had called him because I was afraid I had lost my family, my husband and my 3-year-old daughter. They were gone and I was sure I had driven them away by staying out all night once again, coming home drunk once again, and passing out on the floor of our apartment.

This was my bottom, thinking I had lost them, waking to find them gone. And it was the best thing that could have happened to me. Because of their absence, I made that call, and the person I was calling, a boyfriend from before my marriage, had since gotten sober and knew the score. "Maybe it's your drinking," he said, when I told him I thought I was losing my family. He directed me to my first AA meeting, the first one I was going to for myself, that is.

As Susan said, we had been exposed to AA by our mom, Gloria D. She got sober in the 1960s when I was 13 and just starting my drinking journey. She had a few slips along the way, seven in fact, but she was sober almost 23 years when she died in 2019. I told her I was 90 days sober at the wake for my grandfather, her father. She cried with happiness and gave me her copy of *One Day at a Time*.

My sister got sober eight years later. I know this was the best gift either of us have given to our mother—or to ourselves.

The family disease was there in my marriage too. My husband got sober four years after me and our nephew found his way to AA a few years later after almost dying from a brain bleed incurred after hitting his head in a drunken fall. Even my daughter was sober for a period of time. I hope that someday, should she need to, she returns.

There's really no way to compare the fun I have today with my idea of fun when I was drinking. I laugh from a deeper place. It surprised me the first time I really laughed in sobriety. It felt new, different. I have fun working with others on projects we all love. I have fun getting to the other side of things that scare me. I have fun sitting with my sister or an AA friend, listening, baring our souls. I have fun gazing at a sunset, listening to the rain, walking, reading, learning, enjoying silences. There's no comparison.

Susan and Lynda C.
New York, New York

Family Tree

From: ***Dear Grapevine***
October 2020

I'm an alcoholic. It's the most important aspect of me. It helps give me humility, reminds me of who I am exactly, brings change into focus and delivers peace.

My grandmother was one of the first 100 women in AA, and my mom came in 1979—two amazing women. I got to AA myself in 1989.

My grandmother would say, "When you pick up that first drink, you lose the power to choose." My mother often says, "Peace at any price." They also told me that the "ism" part of alcoholism stands for "I'm Sponsoring Myself." What I say when I'm in fear is ... I'm thinking only about me. When I'm in faith, I'm thinking about you.

I'm so grateful for the AA women in my family tree. Thank you, AA, for keeping the doors open.

Maura D.
Hot Springs, South Dakota

The Reclaimed Turkey Carver

December 1975

On Thanksgiving, the turkey is the main event in my family household. When I was a boy, the art of carving the bird was passed on to me by my father. But later, my drunkenness on Thanksgiving kept me from carving the bird, and I found myself being fed on a tray in front of the television set—so I could watch my football games, I thought. I learned later that my banishment was by request of family friends who dined with us on Thanksgiving Day and felt my eating habits did not enhance their meal.

After 11 months in AA, I was asked to carve the family bird for friends and family on Thanksgiving. On my way to the kitchen, I counted noses and plates to see if I was eating with everyone else, and found I was. As I was carving the turkey, I started to laugh, and I laughed until I cried and laughed some more.

It is a nice feeling to be welcomed back to the dining-room table and even nicer to be reinstated in the turkey-carving department. Maybe, through AA and my Higher Power, I can carve the bird this Thanksgiving and Christmas, too.

You know, I do not remember who won the football games last Thanksgiving, but I know who carved the turkey in my house, and for this, I am grateful.

Dick B.
Fort Myers, Florida

CHAPTER THREE

The Joys of Sponsorship

Loving, trusting and helping each other recover, one on one

"None of us would be here today if somebody hadn't taken the time to explain things to us, to give us a little pat on the back."
Dr. Bob, "Farewell Talk," July 30, 1950

Helping someone find the light of sobriety is a true gift. And as this chapter shows, sponsors have a way of instilling gratitude in the most stubborn of alcoholics. Although Tom L. laughs at the way his first sponsor Delmar pronounces alcoholic "alky-holic" in his story "I Laughed, He Laughed," he learns how to pray on his knees and humbly clean up after meetings.

Ultimately, gratitude and long-term sobriety are the results of this unlikeliest of pairings. In "I Want What She Has," Terri T. describes her return to prison at the age of 43, full of anger and fear, only to find a sponsor behind bars who convinces her of two seemingly irreconcilable facts: That she was an alcoholic and that there was hope for her. She writes, "I'm so grateful for the women who led me to AA, to the women who came before me and to the women I now get to help."

Gratitude is also on Sandy W.'s mind, as a man with not one, but three, temporary sponsors. In his story "3 Guys, 4 Miracles," he is taught that he can live life on life's terms and find true thankfulness for the miracles that he experiences on a regular basis.

I Laughed, He Laughed

May 2020

Delmar had a Southern Georgia drawl like nobody else. He used to say, "alky-holic." He was a big man with a big smile and a mischievous twinkle in his eye, along with a hearty laugh. He loved AA and he did as much Twelfth Step work as anyone I have known in the program. As he put it, he was "out chasing drunks most nights." In addition to his day job as a construction engineer, he ran an aftercare program for a large treatment outfit. His energy was boundless.

Delmar was my first sponsor. He sponsored a lot of men. I asked him to help me because he was friendly and always laughing and he was one of the regulars of my group. He just smiled when I asked him and said, "Call me tomorrow."

I did. And I quickly learned that he was serious about the Steps and serious about service work. At the same time, he did not push. If I was serious, fine. If I did not follow his "suggestions," that was fine too. He had other men to work with and other things to do.

At the end of the meeting after I asked him to sponsor me, he said, "We're going to wash ashtrays." Cigarette smoke used to hang in layers at our meetings. There were a lot of ashtrays to collect off the tables, wash and put up. As we did that nasty chore, we talked. Sometimes I talked and he listened. Sometimes I asked questions I was too shy to bring up in the meeting and he answered. Sometimes we just talked. That was precious time.

The end of the month rolled around and Delmar said, "We're going to the district GSR breakfast this Sunday." That's where I met folks from our area. Then when January came, he announced, "We're going to the state assembly next Saturday and Sunday."

I was one bewildered member in that sea of faces, but I began to learn how this thing we call AA is put together. At the end of what seemed an interminable stretch of time, I finally got my 90-day chip. That's when Delmar's directions changed. "You're going to chair the meetings next month," he told me. But he was right there at my elbow to help me out.

Delmar taught me the most important lesson about being married that a few marriage therapists missed: "One person cannot have an argument." That was, and still is, absolutely profound.

He taught me about prayer. Early on, I heard him speak at our group. He shared about coming home early from work and finding his wife on her knees in their living room praying. He was shocked. "What if our neighbors saw you like that?" he asked. Her response was to the point. "What better way would I want them to see me than on my knees praying?"

I was praying by that time. Still, it took me a while longer to hit my knees. "Boy, the only thing you need to know about God is that there is one and you ain't him," Delmar would say. Later, when I complained and complained some more about my job and my boss and my life, he told me, "Turn in your 'God card.'" He had to tell me that several times. Surrender was a hard concept for me.

The first time I heard Delmar's story was at our home group. He grew up very poor and he had been through some difficult experiences. Despite that, he had gotten an education and he was married and had two sons. Then his oldest was killed in a car wreck late one night. Many of us in the room had no idea what he had gone through and what he lived with daily. Here was an affable, friendly man who was always smiling and laughing and telling stories, generous with his time and his help. He did not seem to have a problem in the world.

Today, I know that every alcoholic who makes it to AA has seen some heartache, but I was stunned when I heard Delmar speak that night. He knew about pain. He understood.

Delmar called the Fourth Step "taking out the garbage." I was five months into sobriety before I was willing to do one. He gave me instructions and I went home and prayed and wrote. I did that each day after work for about a week. Finally, when I was done, I called him and went over to his house. We sat in his backyard under the trees. After we prayed together, I read him that mess, every bit of it. It took a while, but he did me the favor of staying awake. And he did not throw me out of his yard.

I heard a speaker at an AA roundup one time tell the crowd that a Fourth Step was "not a list of filthy, nasty things." My first one was a list of filthy, nasty things. But Delmar was unfazed. He shared a few things himself and we even laughed a little. Then he sent me home to think about what I had just done for the past hour.

Was I relieved, but spiritually lightened? No, I was just glad it was over. But something in me had changed that afternoon under the trees in his yard.

Delmar also taught me the importance of sticking with it. At almost five years sober, I was doing well. Life was good and busy. My family loved me, my job was good, and I was sober. I just didn't come around my home group or the meetings very much. I had not seen Delmar in weeks. Then one morning, as I got ready for work, I realized that I hated everything and everyone. I was "restless, irritable, and discontented" for no good reason whatsoever. I called Delmar.

He met me for lunch at a fried chicken joint on the southside of town. He was sitting over on the side. When I got my tray and came over, he did not even give me time enough to sit down. "How many meetings are you making each week?" he asked. "And when was the last time you did a Fourth and Fifth Step?"

I laughed sheepishly, and he laughed, and I sat down and ate my chicken. Then I rejoined the AA program and became involved with my home group. I wrote a second Fourth Step and saw Delmar for the Fifth again.

Not long after that, Delmar retired from working road construction for the state and moved to another town. I still saw him at workshops, intergroup, the state assembly and our annual roundup, which he helped start. Eventually I got another sponsor. Delmar had developed breathing problems from all the road work he supervised.

He stayed as active as he could for as long as he could.

The last time I saw Delmar was at his AA birthday. A friend called and asked me to speak. I was honored and scared I would say something stupid.

In that small clubhouse, Delmar sat at a table so close to the front I literally reached across and shook his hand when I got up to speak. I have no idea, of course, what I said, but even on oxygen, he laughed a lot.

When I finished, he hugged me, and I told him that I loved him. I still do. He died a few months later.

What do you owe your sponsor? What do I owe mine? In a very real sense, my life. Because of that man my life has been a very good one.

Tom L.
Albany, Georgia

7 Hours and a Box of Tissues

May 2025

I did my first Fifth Step with my sponsor Neena. I had about eight months sober. It was the best day of my life. I became a different person that day. Two weeks before we read the Big Book up to the Fourth Step. Then Neena said, "For the next two weeks I want you to work on your Fourth Step for 15 minutes every day." We prepared my notebook like it shows in the Big Book with columns. I was to write at the top of each page FEAR (False Evidence Appearing Real). She said for me to call her when I needed help.

Over the next two weeks I would call her when my heart was breaking or the memories felt too difficult. My sponsor would listen, and when I finished talking she would say, "OK, now stop crying and go to a meeting." Or she would say, "These memories can't hurt you; you've already been through that situation. It's now on paper." Then she'd hang up. "Feel your feelings and go to a meeting," she kept telling me.

The day finally came to do my Fifth Step. Neena came to my apartment and we both got on our knees and read the Third Step Prayer out loud out of our Big Books while holding hands. I felt like God was lifting me up. I knew in that moment I would be OK. I've been chasing that feeling every day since.

Neena and I sat on my back patio for seven hours that day. We went through three packs of cigarettes and a box of tissues doing my Fifth Step. She gave me her full attention and never blinked an eye at some of the things I told her. She didn't judge me or criticize. She listened and gave me compassion and love. I still cannot recall anyone up to that point in my life ever giving me that much love and attention. Her whole motive was just to help me get and stay sober.

When we finished she suggested I lie down for an hour and think of the work I had done so far. If anything came to me that we didn't get to, we could do it immediately. Nothing came, so we were both satisfied that I had done my first Fourth and Fifth Step thoroughly.

After we finished going through the Big Book, Neena moved to Georgia to start a new business. She and I are still in contact today. I call her often and she usually answers with "Hey sweet girl," or, "Hey, baby girl, what's up?" Her voice is like magic to my ears when we speak. It makes my heart feel like it's exploding with gratitude. She's still my rock. She knows me and understands me best because she took the time to listen to my Fifth Step. I can't wait to do the same for other women.

The best part of Steps Four and Five is the time I spent with my sponsor. Sponsors can help us see our part in all our resentments. Today I can see my part pretty quickly (well, sometimes slowly). It helps me be able to make an amend right away. I get to have a quality life, the kind my Higher Power wants me to have. Thank you Neena and mostly Alcoholics Anonymous.

Tina W.
Jupiter, Florida

17 Years of Hope

June 2020

I attended my first AA meeting in 1981 in Alhambra, California. It was a blessing. I was 19.

I'm writing to share my gratitude about being able to carry the AA message and my experience, strength and hope to another woman who's incarcerated. My friend in prison had a sentence of 15 to 30 years. She's a bit older and sober several years more than me. Pretty darn amazing. The General Service Office in New York sent me her address during her first year in prison. That was more than 17 years ago.

So for these many years, our letters have traveled back and forth from an old farmhouse in rural Kansas to a mega state prison in Arizona. We've discussed Steps, resentments, solutions, Traditions, bills, goals, the Slogans and God. We've sometimes even discussed making desserts.

Sentiments of love are exchanged, as we pass letters about the lighter and harder parts of life in sobriety ... things like the death of family members, running over the dog, making my first cheesecake, not getting to enough meetings, getting fatter, getting thinner, getting beaten up by a cellmate—and the valuable lesson of easy does it.

AA taught me that action helps me stay sober. For the two of us, action is picking up a pen, getting paper and a stamp and writing an address on an envelope. For her, pens, paper, stamps and envelopes are luxuries. They are not easy to get.

One day at a time, she and I have racked up a lot of postage miles in these 17 years. Because she has more sobriety, she has often sponsored me toward a fresher perspective and greater serenity as we trudge this road. Yes, it's possible to walk, talk and write the path of sobriety from the "inside"-out through the mail. It's been one of the most endearing trips in sobriety I have ever taken.

Tess M.
Kansas

3 Guys, 4 Miracles

August 2024

When I first got sober, I had wreckage of my past to deal with. I had warrants out for my arrest, and I was five days away from a final eviction notice. I was also hiding my truck to keep it from being repossessed. And on top of that, every time I got a cold or felt ill, I thought I might have HIV because I had all the morals of a tomcat when it came to women.

Here's what happened. I got lucky because I got sobered up at a clubhouse in San Antonio. Right away three AA guys snagged me right out of my first meeting. They had between one year and 18 months sober and were all in their early 30s like me. They sat me down and helped me get through my first few days sober. They became my first temporary sponsors.

At the time I was living on coffee, orange juice and peanut butter cups and going to every AA meeting I could. I went to four or five a day for the first couple days as the fog was lifting and my real-world issues were materializing at lightning speed.

One day I was in a pickle, freaking out, when my three sponsors got together, held an intervention and started telling me what to do. They told me, "Sandy, don't think. Your best thinking got you here. We'll be doing your thinking for you until you get your head together." Here's what they suggested:

Rent: They said to pray and ask God for guidance. Then to go to my apartment manager and tell her the truth. "Are you freaking crazy?" I replied. They told me to go to her and apologize for my past lies and behavior. Then tell her I'm in AA and trying to get straightened out. Promise her that on payday I will pay the upcoming month's rent and in two weeks when I get paid, I'll pay half of the past due rent and finish paying it off by the middle of next month. So off I went. I said and did exactly as these guys told me to do.

Here's what the apartment manager said after I had my talk with her: "Oh Sandy, that's great news. Everyone here likes you so much. We were so afraid we were going to get news that you were dead or locked up somewhere. Sure, I will work with you." Then she hugged me! Miracle No.1!

Next were the warrants for bounced checks. Same process. My three guys suggested I pray and ask God for guidance—then go to the constable, tell the truth and offer to work out a payment plan. Worst case I'd go to jail and get three hots and a cot until I went to court. Same thing happened. After I spoke with him, the constable said, "You're going to AA? That's great son. We don't want to arrest you, but you will have to pay these checks off through my office over time. If you don't, you will go to jail." Miracle No. 2!

The truck, same deal. Tell the truth and pray about it. I called up the finance company and told them where the truck was going to be or that I'd bring it back. They told me to just make a payment and keep the truck for now. And wouldn't you know? The next day I walked into work and my boss said, "Hey Sandy, I got good news. Corporate says you can use a company car." So I gave my truck back to the bank and used a company car. I like to believe this was a God thing. I think it definitely was. Miracle No. 3!

Finally, I was pretty sick in early sobriety. All the time I had a runny nose, headaches, diarrhea, body aches, and was tired and depressed. My three sponsors said, "Sandy, go to the county health clinic. Tell them the truth and see if they'll run some tests." So I did that. It turned out I had the flu on top of detoxing from alcohol and everything else. And I didn't have an STD. Miracle No. 4! Peace of mind.

I can't thank these three guys enough for helping me and telling me what to do. That first year I thoroughly worked the Steps as best I could, and I discovered what many before me already knew: That the Steps work for resolving a multitude of things, and the things the Steps do not resolve could be resolved through outside help and a strong personal relationship with a Higher Power.

I've been in AA now for 32 years with no slips and with one very short dry drunk when I stopped going to meetings and doing service work. Oh, but that's another story!

Sandy W.
Odessa, Florida

I Want What She Has

June 2025

I returned to prison for the third time in March of 2011. I never was very good at learning my lessons the first time. I was 43 years old and had been serving time either locked up in women's prison, in community corrections or on state supervision since I was 21. Every time I got released from a facility I would go back to the bottle. My return to institutions came faster each time. I had been lying about my drinking and using for so long that even I believed the lie that I didn't have a problem. Oblivious to the consequences my drinking caused, I thought I was just unlucky and claimed I was being targeted by the Department of Corrections.

Alcohol was the only solution I had to living then. I couldn't imagine what life would be like without the ease and comfort I found in a bottle. I spent so much time and energy hiding my drinking because it seemed the only way to survive. When I did get locked up I would turn to a concoction of psychiatric medications to alter how I felt. I really thought I couldn't live life sober. I had to alter my perception and fill that giant hole in my heart. I was fueled with fear and anger.

But this time when I got locked up, something was different. I knew in the core of my being that if I didn't do something, if I didn't change, I was going to die. I got on my knees and asked God for help. However, going to prison again was not exactly the help I had in mind.

Luckily, at this women's prison there was an in-house AA meeting on Monday nights. At my first meeting there I watched these outside women volunteers as they arrived and walked into our dayroom. They appeared to be so happy. Their cheerfulness didn't seem forced or fake. It was one of the first real things I can remember that night. I did not want to participate in the meeting because that would mean I had to admit I had a problem and then that would mean I wouldn't be able to drink when I got out. So I just watched. And I continued watching these AA women every week for 18 months.

My roommate's name was Kacy, and she was a member of the group. She had been going to AA meetings on the outside before she was sentenced and her sponsor wrote her letters and visited the prison once a week. I was lucky to get mail once a month, while Kacy had an entire AA community supporting her. I found myself longing to be part of what she had, but my fear and pride wouldn't let me ask her how she did it because I was afraid what she did wouldn't work for me. I was not willing to let my deepest, darkest secret out. I still couldn't fathom a life without drinking.

Kacy never preached to me or thumped her Big Book at me. She just walked around every day with a dignity and grace I had a hard time understanding. She told me many stories about herself and what had happened to her. She told me she was free on the inside, even here in prison. I watched her and her sponsor going through the Big Book in the chapel. I found myself feeling jealous over the joy she had. She had something I wanted so deeply, but I was so afraid to ask for it.

Not long after that, I was moved to a community corrections program, and luckily a few months later, Kacy was transferred to the same facility. A few days later I met Moe, who would become my first real sponsor. When Moe sat down across the table from me and started telling me about her drinking and her thinking, I was able to completely relate for one of the first times in my life. I now knew I was an alcoholic and was convinced there was hope for me. Moe's life sounded better than mine did. She had the things I silently dreamed about. Her relationship with her kids had been restored, she had worked at the same job for a couple of years, her bills were paid, and she was content with her life. I had never felt content with anything. I was willing to do anything Moe suggested.

Soon my life started to get better. I began to find hope. The secrets that I had buried deep inside were no longer wounds to drink over, but became stepping stones to healing. I would have never received the miracle of AA if it had been forced upon me. Stubborn defiance would have kept me out of the rooms. It was attraction, not promotion, that worked for me.

I'm so grateful for the women who led me to AA, to the women who came before me and to the women I now get to help.

Terri T.
Billings, Montana

Team Bob

From: ***Dear Grapevine***
February 2020

A while back, I fell and broke my femur bone. Not good for a 100-year-old alcoholic. I ended up in a nursing facility for two months.

Finally, Jim, who I sponsor, came in and said, "Bob, I'm getting you out!" I was ecstatic. Jim then wheeled me out to the patio. My daughter and my three AA sponsees were there. "We're a team," Jim said, "and we have a plan to get you home and cared for."

I can't tell you how the return home felt. My sponsee Robert moved in to stay with me at night. At 6 A.M., a fellow AA came in to care for me until 9 A.M. Then another sponsee would care for me from 3 to 6 P.M., when Robert returned home. My sponsees are good cooks, so I was well-fed. I had a house cleaner as well as someone to do the laundry. My lady friend of 14 years spent the weekends with me.

I now need less care and I can cook by microwave. When I'm alone,

I wear a 911 call badge. Being home and living a close to normal life is a true gift from my Higher Power.

My 72 years in AA got me these wonderful sponsees. My grateful heart thanks all my caregivers and dear AA friends.

Bob M.
La Mesa, Calif.

Starting Over

January 2025

When I was new to the AA program, I did everything that was suggested. I read the Big Book, chose a home group, started working the Steps and got a sponsor. I think I believed that if I didn't get a sponsor, my home group would find out and I'd be chastised, perhaps even "fired" from AA.

I chose a lovely older woman with about 20 years of sobriety to be my sponsor. She was gentle and kind and asked very little of me (which worked well for me at that time). Her main request was that I call her once a week. Sometimes I did, sometimes I didn't. We all know that 700-pound telephone!

In time, I moved away from that area and my first sponsor died. Over the years, I sometimes asked others to sponsor me, but I rarely utilized them except when I occasionally felt the need to do some specific Step work.

When I celebrated my 20th AA birthday, a remarkable thing happened. I wasn't cocky, I wasn't proud, but I was aware of what a big milestone that was. Many things in the world and in my life had changed in 20 years. I felt my Higher Power saying to me, "Yes, you're right, 20 years is amazing. It's a generation, a significant accomplishment—period. Now, let's start all over again."

I had been without a sponsor for quite a while, so I took this as a nudge from my Higher Power to get one. I asked a woman in my home group, and she agreed.

My life has not been the same since. Every single week for almost eight years she and I sat at our kitchen tables working our programs and enjoying each other's fellowship. We worked the Steps. We read through the entire Big Book out loud together. Then we read *Twelve Steps and Twelve Traditions.* We talked about our daily lives and the challenges therein and shared how we tried to practice the principles of the program in all our affairs.

I found myself immersed in the program at a depth I had not experienced before. Small wonder then, that as a result of all this work, my spiritual program, my relationship with my Higher Power, grew deeper as well.

Suddenly women began asking me to sponsor them. It seemed that working my own program with new energy and depth began to show in how I lived. My program came alive, and I was given the opportunity to pass it on.

I love having a sponsor; it's an amazingly unique relationship. Today, although I have again moved away, I still talk with her every week. There's tremendous value in having someone know all about me. I have shared those huge things with her I swore I would never tell anyone, then those lesser things I was embarrassed to share, then those smaller things that seem too trivial to share, until I finally had shared all of me.

As I approach 29 years of sobriety, I think I finally have no secrets left. My sponsor knows me so well by now that I can bring any concern or question to her, and she understands me and the journey I've been on. With her, I am known and accepted just as I am.

And I also love sponsoring. As I take those I work with through the Steps, whether they are newcomers or veterans of the program, I learn so much from their journeys.

Our Big Book promises that when I work with others, "Life will take on new meaning." I'm profoundly grateful for those who took the time to pass their program on to me and for the opportunity to do the same.

Anonymous
Wilsonville, Oregon

CHAPTER FOUR

Getting Through Tough Times

Being grateful for a program, the tools and a loving Fellowship to get through adversity

Once we get sober, life keeps happening, as this chapter illustrates. But we get through things, we stay sober and it often makes us stronger.

Chuck H., in his extraordinary story "In My Darkest Hour," was sitting in his 6:00 A.M. AA meeting, grateful to be surrounded by those he loves. Yet just a few hours before, his beloved wife had died unexpectedly. "At no time did I get angry with God. ... The feeling I had was one of gratitude for the 51 years my wife and I had together," he writes. "I was grateful to God for the sobriety he had given me."

Gratitude in the face of daunting circumstances is a constant theme of the stories in this chapter. Debra B. describes her frightening experiences in "Faith & Flashlights," where she rides out a powerful Florida hurricane with her Big Book, her Bible and her flashlight. "I have never felt so close to my Higher Power as at that time," she writes. "I really never felt alone."

Then there's "A Grateful Holiday" from John K., whose drinking destroys a life that he says was "like a Hollywood set." When he finds his way to an AA meeting, the sound of people describing themselves as "grateful alcoholics" drives him crazy. Grateful? How can that be? But after almost a year in the program, he stood up at a meeting and said: "Hi, I'm John. I'm a grateful alcoholic."

In My Darkest Hour

February 2020

The December 2006 issue of Grapevine included an article I wrote about my recovery and my marriage. In my story, I told of how I learned to apply the Steps of AA to my marriage and to my everyday life. Upon the suggestion of a loving sponsor, I learned how to contribute to that marriage and how to turn it over to the care of God. The name of my story was, "Whose Marriage Is It Anyway?"

Around my one year AA birthday in April of 1984, my marriage didn't just change, it blossomed. I felt as though God reached out and touched us and turned our troubled marriage into something beautiful. I saw this as a living example of the Twelve Steps working in my life.

The article closed with me celebrating five years of sobriety and us celebrating 25 years of marriage. My wife Dorothea insisted that we go out and buy new wedding rings and renew our wedding vows.

For the next 25 years, we were walking through life together. Friday nights became "date night," as my wife loved to go to AA speaker meetings. In April of 2014, I celebrated 30 years of sobriety. In October, my wife and I celebrated 50 years of marriage. One more time, my wife wanted to go out and get new wedding rings and renew our vows. We did exactly that.

We had retired by this time and traveled all over the country and the world. I found meetings on the back roads of the U.S. and in the remote parts of Canada and Alaska. I got to meetings around the world, including Australia, Argentina, Germany and Turkey.

In 2016, just five days before my 32nd year of sobriety, my wife suffered a massive brain hemorrhage. Once I recognized the signs that something was wrong, that she was experiencing some sort of attack, I intuitively knew what to do. I immediately called 911. Then I called my daughter. Then my sponsor. Next I called an AA friend who lived near me, as I knew better than to drive myself. The paramedics were in the house and attending to Dorothea within five minutes of the original call. She was in the hospital in less than 10 minutes.

Half an hour later, the doctor told my daughter and me that we needed to "just let her go," to allow God to take her. Those words still ring in my ears ... "Just let her go."

Right then, I gave my wife over to the care of God. My sponsor, my daughter and my AA friend were with me in those final moments of Dorothea's life. I was not alone. My sponsor gathered me into his arms and held onto me as I cried.

At 3:05 A.M., on the 19th of April, on the very day of my 32nd year of sobriety, God took my wife home. I was able to kiss her on the forehead and thank her for being my wife for 51 years.

At 5:00 A.M., I parked my car in front of a building where I knew a 6:00 A.M. AA meeting would be held. I placed a small sign on the windshield of my car with the words: "Wake me at 6 o'clock. I need a meeting." I was awakened by an AA member and entered that meeting as a widower. The outpouring of love and caring I felt there was unbelievable. I was not alone that morning.

Later, we had a "celebration of life" for my wife and the response from my AA community was overwhelming. At no time did I get angry with God. At no time did I feel alone and at no time did I feel afraid. The feeling I had was one of gratitude for the 51 years my wife and I had together, and I was grateful to God for the sobriety he had given me.

The Twelve Steps and AA gave me a life I would have never known. Even in my darkest hour, God and the Fellowship of AA was with me. And thanks to AA, I was never alone.

Chuck H.
Laguna Woods, California

Accepting the Road Ahead

February 2024

Miracles have been happening in my life and they started happening on October 9, 1986. That's the day I admitted I was an alcoholic and needed help. I had been confronted about my drinking on the job and was sent home from work. I was told to contact the company's human resources office. They recommended I go into treatment and start attending AA. I did what was suggested and went to my first meeting the next day. Miracle No. 1 had just occurred.

I didn't drink and went to another meeting the next day. Miracle No. 2 is that my sobriety has continued for the past 32 years.

I've grown old in this program while experiencing all the joys and sorrows of life. My most challenging time in sobriety came the day my husband was diagnosed with pancreatic cancer. Most of us know this is a death sentence, and being a registered nurse working in surgery, I had an idea of the journey before us. I was filled with fear, denial and anger. How could this be happening?

Our journey began with my husband and I praying together. Dan had 25 years of sobriety and I had 20 years. We both knew we were powerless and that our Higher Power was in charge. We needed to follow directions, listen to the information given to us, pray, go to AA meetings and talk to our sponsors. We needed to allow each other to process this news at our own pace and in our own way.

My husband was a very private man and he prayed quietly in silence. I'm a vocal open book. I needed to talk, cry and plan for the future. We respected each other and our own journeys. We accomplished these goals with humble gratitude for our Higher Power and our lives in AA.

Dan accepted this diagnosis and the fight ahead of him. He did this with quiet dignity and gave himself permission to ask others for help. He continued living life with courage and his serenity inspired the family to walk with him on this path. We were not a "glum lot," as we found joy in each other. We were present for each moment, the good and bad ones, knowing that "this too shall pass."

I was so full of fear, I cried all the time. I did most of this when I was away from Dan. My drive to and from work was 45 minutes each way, perfect crying time. Surgery, chemo and radiation were devastating his body. My sweet husband did not complain and asked very little of me. Words cannot describe the pain I felt watching my loved one die. I know God carried each of us just as described in the poem "Footprints in the Sand." Dan and I did not drink and we were doing the best we could each day, but I was sure I would not survive without him. Dan was my best friend, confidant and lover. He took care of everything, such as bills and finances.

One day I asked him, "Who's going to hold my hand?" His reply, "Squeeze your hands. I will have one and God will have the other." I continue to do this 12 years later and it always makes me feel like a child between parents holding me up as they swing me.

All my self-centered feelings were brought front and center. I wanted to die with Dan. I did not want to be left behind. I prayed daily to die and received the same answer—no. One day I was out walking, asking once again to die and getting the same answer, so I screamed, "All right, I'll live, but I'm not happy about it!" Acceptance is not always pretty or gentle, but it's the only way I know to peace and serenity. Now that that was settled, I could give love, support, encouragement and yes, even joy to Dan, our family and friends.

The program guided us through admitting our powerlessness, gaining a measure of sanity through our Higher Powers, literally turning our lives and wills over. Both of us continued to do inventories and promptly acknowledged our wrongs and we became closer to God, even when we did not understand our journey. We were given a spiritual awareness as a result of the Steps, enabling us to help other alcoholics.

Dan continued to go to AA meetings as long as he could. His friends brought meetings to our home when he could no longer go to meetings.

We comforted our children and friends and Dan told me he would be waiting for me. If we can believe in beautiful deaths, his death certainly qualifies. It was physically difficult, but spiritually beautiful. My husband died 18 months after his diagnosis. We both tried to live each day to its fullest. We treasured our time and thanked God for giving it to us.

Today I'm alive and well. I'm grateful my Higher Power did not grant my request to die. I have wonderful friends in the rooms of AA. I'm able to be a grownup with responsibilities (pay bills, take care of problems). I have been given the gift of watching our grandchildren grow into wonderful young adults. I can share memories of Grampa because I'm sober and alive.

My journey is not unique, but it's mine. I do not know the end of my story, but I do know I won't be alone and God will take care of me. I see the miracles that have occurred and I know they'll continue to occur in my life as long as I'm sober.

Helen C.
Rockwood, Tennessee

Faith & Flashlights

February 2024

I thought I was prepared. I boarded up the windows, and I planned to cover the French doors, but that didn't work out. The power went out about 11:30 A.M., but I was able to talk to my son on the phone, getting storm updates until about 1:00 P.M. Then the phone cut off. That scared me, as I wondered when, or if, I would ever talk to my son again.

As the wind picked up and I started to see our fence fly away and the trees go down, I decided to seek refuge in the bedroom closet with my kitty. I prayed for our safety, as the wind and rain were so bad you could no longer see out the window. The rain made the view outside look like gray fog.

During the storm, I periodically walked through the house to check on things and I saw that both French doors were buckling. In the bedroom, I moved the oak armoire in front of the bedroom doors and wedged a recliner chair against both the front door and French doors in the living room to secure them.

The wood covering the window in the office had blown off and water was pouring in. At first glance, I thought the window was broken, but the water was streaming in through the seams. Rainwater was pouring in over the doors. I tried to wipe it up with towels and soon every towel in my house was wet. I tried to use buckets and could not possibly catch the quantity of water that was coming in.

All I could do was cry, as I was powerless over this scene. I was frightened and devastated. I asked God to get me through this storm and I returned to the closet, as it was safer.

After about four hours, the hurricane was finally over. Neighbors met on the street to compare damage and make sure everyone was OK. We had no power or water. I went to bed early and prayed and read my Big Book to help me accept what had happened. I knew if I just kept praying, God would get me through this disaster.

The next day I attempted to get out of the neighborhood, but was blocked by downed electrical wires. I started to pick up the thousands of shingles and tree limbs in my yard, which seemed like an impossible task for one person. It was like eating an elephant. I did it one bite at a time.

Later that day one of my son's friends appeared in his uniform in a State of Florida truck. He was able to get through the rubble while he was on duty. I just knew that God had sent him to let me know everything was going to be OK. I was able to call my son on his phone. He made sure I had enough food and that my house was safe.

The third day two of my son's friends came by and checked on me and helped me move some heavy, water-soaked boxes from my shed, and again I was able to call my son on their phone, as they had service. I just knew this was a God thing and I was so grateful that these guys were being sent to me, as it was so hard to be alone through all this.

Later that afternoon I was able to get out to see two AA friends and they had a generator, so I had a cup of coffee, which tasted so good! Seeing my friends made me feel much better and I didn't feel so alone anymore.

Only main roads were open, so travel was limited. The rest of the streets were blocked by downed trees and power lines. It was scary to drive over the power lines and weave in and out of the trees. I missed having contact with my sponsor and AA meetings.

On the fourth day I was able to get to my church, and what a wonderful feeling that was. Not quite a substitute for AA, but the God presence was there for me. Phone service was weak and faded in and out so calls could not be depended on to go through or stay connected for an entire conversation. I was able to receive texts, but could not send them out. I could see on my phone that my friends were having a text conversation asking if anyone had heard from me, but I couldn't answer!

On the fifth day I got to speak with my sponsor on the phone. And I finally got to an AA meeting a week after the storm, out at Panama City Beach. Most of the clubhouses or buildings where the AA meetings were held in town were damaged and not holding meetings yet. It was not long though before most were meeting in temporary locations or in their damaged clubhouses while they rebuilt them. The two things that got me through the aftermath of the hurricane were my Big Book and my Bible. I did not have meetings and regular phone contact with others, but I had contact with my Higher Power. I would pick up either book at any time during the day when I felt worn out and empty. At night when I went to bed I would read by flashlight in the sweltering heat until I fell asleep.

I have never felt so close to my Higher Power as at that time. I knew he would take care of me and get me through it, and he did. I really never felt alone. He sent people to help me all along the way and continues to do so today. He gives me the strength to endure this journey I'm still on. Even months after the hurricane I was still not back in my home, but the light at the end of the tunnel slowly got brighter and brighter.

And through it all, I continued to pray every morning and every night and attend AA meetings daily. Thank you, AA.

Debra B.
Panama City, Florida

A Grateful Holiday

January 2020

My drinking had gone from being a way to escape life's pressures to a long, slow descent into hell. But the end came quickly, a few weeks after one fateful Christmas.

If you saw my life a couple of months before that, it seemed pretty good as long as you didn't look too closely. I was married to a smart, beautiful, funny woman. I had a great job, a nice house in a trendy neighborhood and lots of shiny toys. I spent that Christmas on a private island in the Caribbean. And I was being served 20-year-old scotch in crystal tumblers by smiling waiters in white linen jackets.

My life was like a Hollywood set. From a distance it was impressive, but up close you could see that it was hollow, nothing more than painted canvas. I was physically exhausted and emotionally and spiritually bankrupt. Financial ruin was not far behind.

I had convinced my wife that this trip would be a new beginning. We would escape the mad whirlwind of Christmas back home in Toronto and put our relationship back on track. I swore, for the umpteenth time, that things would be different. But I simply couldn't stop drinking and I hated myself for it. It was killing both of us. The more clearly I saw the pain in her eyes, the more I drank to escape my guilt and shame. The worst part was that the booze had stopped working. All I could think about was killing myself, but I lacked the courage.

When we returned home after New Year's Eve, the whole house of cards came tumbling down. By the end of January, my marriage was over. I was living in my car and my employer was preparing to get rid of me.

I crawled into my first AA meeting at what would become my home group, The Beaches Group, in Toronto. I was a broken man. My God, I thought, this is what it's come to, Alcoholics Anonymous. How desperate can you be? I should have killed myself, I thought.

I was not an ideal newcomer. I was angry, argumentative and, despite everything, full of self-centered pride. When I heard people introduce themselves as "grateful alcoholics," it was like nails being dragged over a chalkboard. But I had nowhere else to go so I kept coming back.

I kept telling people I was "different." Finally, someone told me to read the story "Physician, Heal Thyself!" in the back of the Big Book. I'm not a doctor, but for the first time I actually identified with the writer. Those words on the first page of that story, "the skid row of success," fairly jumped off the page at me. That phrase cracked my shell of pride just enough to let in the healing sunlight of humility.

The earth completed another orbit of the sun. Christmas was a few days away once again. I took stock of my life. There was no private island in the Caribbean this Christmas. I was living in a one-room apartment with a hot plate and a view of a brick wall six feet away, but I had a warm, dry place to sleep and food to eat.

I was going through divorce proceedings, but thanks to the work I had begun on the Steps, I was able to accept responsibility for the damage I had done to that relationship. I had serious financial issues to deal with, but I was dealing with them. My employer had decided to give me one more chance and seemed pleased with the results. Best of all, though I still had moments of fear and uncertainty, I also had moments of serenity. Hope had become a very real part of my life.

The week before Christmas, my home group holds a candlelit gratitude meeting. It's normally a speaker meeting, but for this one evening everyone is given a few moments to share. I wondered what I could possibly say. I thought back to that first meeting 11 months before. I realized that the desperation I had felt was the greatest gift I had ever received. It was the key to a new way of life.

When it was my turn, I simply said, "My name is John. I'm a grateful alcoholic."

And I actually meant it.

John K.
Carleton Place, Ontario

So Worth Living

February 2024

One day in November of 2007, with 22 years of sobriety, I was a passenger in a high-speed motor vehicle accident. A swerving vehicle hit our car, then pushed it into the next lane where another vehicle hit us and we rolled over three times, end over end. I was awake and conscious the whole time, metal crashing repeatedly into pavement at 65 mph. Every time we landed upside down, I expected to die but didn't.

In a matter of minutes, I lost my career, my spouse's career, our home (which had required two incomes to pay the mortgage) and my credit rating (while hospitalized I failed to pay one month's worth of bills and the late notices went into my credit rating, which fell through the floor.) Our new car was demolished. And I went through all that sober. I'm writing this now with 33 years and counting.

The accident caused damage throughout my brain. I lost the ability to filter out background noise. Yet I just went to the California Northern Coastal Area Pre-Conference Assembly as my group's GSR. There were 500 rowdy sober alcoholics in one big room there. I had to wear earplugs the entire time. It was an awesome experience, but totally exhausting.

One limitation resulting from late effects of my traumatic brain injury (momentary losses of consciousness) is that I lost my driving privileges. A great irony is that I never lost my license while drunk and high, though I certainly deserved to get arrested many times. I just never got caught.

Many times I have had to humbly call AA members and ask for rides to meetings. It's so much easier to give help than to ask for it! I've had to practice a lot of acceptance. It helps to remind myself how many rides I've gladly given to others over the years, and how happy it always made me. I'm learning to accept that it's OK to receive, because that provides others the chance to enjoy being the givers.

It took some time to arrange, but I now have regular rides to three AA meetings a week: Monday Meditation, Sebastopol, California (my home group); Thursday Women's Step Study; Friday LGBT Beginners (I call it beginners' tongue in cheek since many in that room have decades of sobriety under their belts.) I get a ride to our district meeting once a month so I'm able to volunteer to be a GSR for my home group.

I'm so grateful to the members who bring me to meetings. I also belong to a closed online AA group. The group has 15,000 members worldwide, so I've been able to spend time online with other sober people anytime I want. None of this was available when I first got sober, so I'm glad I didn't become disabled until late in the day.

I'm also grateful for Grapevine. I love to read it, especially the old issues kept by the groups I attend. In addition to my brain injury, I also suffer from clinical depression, which has worsened. Living with these disabilities has taught me so much about humility, acceptance and gratitude.

It's important to me to reach out and support other members with dual or multiple diagnoses. I'm serving on the committee planning a workshop on mental health in sobriety where I have a very important job. I'm in charge of the food! And I'm planning on getting some real food—not just cookies!

One of the most meaningful things in my life is to sponsor others with dual or multiple diagnoses. We work the Steps together: I get to rework all of the Steps right alongside my sponsees, sharing our experience, strength and hope. We also share our experience with weakness and despair. This is the only way we get to know and trust and inspire each other—so we can heal together. Our cofounder Bill W. also suffered severe depression at times in his sobriety. It didn't make him drink, and with his example, I won't drink either.

Today I belong to what some wiseacre I know calls the "No Matter What Club," and invite my sponsees to join too. We don't drink no matter what. Life is so worth living.

Sarah B.
Sebastopol, California

Up From the Ashes

September 2020

On November 8, 2018, when I had 12 years sober, Paradise, California, a town with 30,000 people two hours north of Sacramento, burned to the ground. Paradise is where I lived.

I woke that morning to red skies and news that the town was being evacuated. Paradise had had fires on its outskirts before. But since my family and I lived very far inside town, I didn't think the fires would ever reach us. We packed several changes of clothes, our laptops, some toiletries and a couple of books (including my Big Book) in case we'd have to stay away for a couple of days.

Then suddenly, the fire was upon us. The neighbor's shed exploded in flames. The wind gusted our way and our back acre went up in a blaze. My husband told me to take our adult son, who has autism, and get out right away.

I left in my old minivan with my son, our cat, one of our dogs and my son's five pet rats in a small travel cage. We joined the procession of cars leaving town. The traffic was bumper to bumper and was often at a standstill.

By the time we got to the main road out of town, everything was on fire. Buildings were collapsing, trees were exploding and emergency personnel were doing their best to keep cars moving in an orderly manner.

People without cars were running down the street, carrying children and pets with blankets over their heads as sparks fell on them. Cars ran out of gas or overheated and had to be abandoned on the road, and we drove around them. The smoky sky was pitch black, illuminated only by headlights and fire and emergency vehicles. It was a surreal and terrifying chaos.

At one point, my son asked me if we were going to be all right and I said, "Yes, I promise." We said the Serenity Prayer and I thanked my Higher Power there wasn't a bottle of vodka under my front seat like there used to be in the old days, nor did I want there to be. I was so glad I wasn't hungover. I was able to be present and effective.

I was so scared each time traffic stopped and we waited to move again. I prayed and kept trying my phone. I had no idea where my husband was. It turned out he had stayed behind and tried, with the garden hose, to put out the fire on our roof. When he realized it was a losing battle, he left in his car with the other two dogs and was diverted down a different road.

Eventually, we cleared the fire and were able to make our way down the hill to the nearby town of Chico, where we spent the night with a fellow AA member, with our whole family (including my husband) and all pets intact. I attended an AA meeting that night and there were several Paradise members there, all of us shell-shocked, crying and holding each other.

Over the next couple of days, we couch surfed with other AA members. Everyone pitched in and cared for our pets, fed us, housed us and clothed us. We lost everything except what we had brought with us. We didn't realize until later that we would never go back home again because our house was completely gone.

Since the the fire, thanks to my amazing home group, we now have a place to live, with furniture and household items. We are slowly rebuilding our lives. People are still living in tents around town, unable to find housing and basic necessities. Local charities have been amazing, and the surrounding communities, including people all over the country, have really come to our aid with donations, support and prayers.

If not for my Higher Power, my program, my sponsees and my home group, I could not have made it through this. It's an amazing example of what service is and a powerful reminder that we don't drink—no matter what.

Carla H.
Chico, California

Acceptance & Gratitude

From: ***Dear Grapevine***
January 2025

I learned about gratitude from a longtimer in Piqua, Ohio. Bob was the guy who always had a joke and a smile on his face.

It was after his wife died from cancer that I heard about the challenges in Bob's life. He had a son killed in Vietnam and a daughter killed by a drunk driver. He also had an adult son in his 30s at home with a disability.

Bob didn't know his sobriety date. He had been in and out of the program for 15 years before he got sober. When his wife passed away he went through the usual stages of grief until he finally came to some acceptance. One day he realized there was something beyond acceptance. He got down on his knees and prayed to God and gave thanks for the years they had together.

Several months ago, I was diagnosed with bone cancer. There is no cure for it at this time, but I'm incredibly grateful to AA, my Higher Power and the wonderful life and family I have.

Thank you Bob, for showing me how important gratitude is, especially at our most difficult moments.

Al A.
Troy, Ohio

What I Know for Sure

February 2025

It was a cool Monday evening in November 1988 when I walked into that men's meeting in Los Altos, California. I had called the San Jose Central Office earlier and asked, "What is it you do?"

Meetings, they said. Yes, they had meetings. Was there one nearby? Yes, there was. Tonight, in fact. They asked if I was having a problem. Would I like someone to come talk with me? That I could answer—no. I didn't need help, and I didn't want someone pestering me with questions and probably asking for money.

At the time, I was drinking a fifth of whatever I could afford daily, rounding out with two-dollar-a-gallon wine. It had taken me 30 years to get to that level of drinking, in which time I had wrecked two marriages, as well as the love of everyone who cared (or tried to care) for me. I also ruined several once-promising careers. The alcohol that had been such a faithful friend and ally since high school days had turned into a demanding tyrant.

I had no idea what AA was or what it did. Something to do with drinking, I figured. Perhaps they could teach me to drink manageably. Perhaps they'd give me some new excuses. Perhaps I'd find a new drinking buddy, someone who drank like me. And so I took a chance and walked into a meeting one minute before it started. Before I could make it to a back row, someone big grabbed my hand and said, "Welcome! We're glad to see you!"

I hadn't heard that in years. Did he know who he was talking to? I was a bum off the street. But I stayed, and by staying I found hope for the first time in forever. Thirty-two years later, I'm still here. Hope endures.

Being college-educated (I'm not sure how I graduated), I have a good vocabulary. AA, however, taught me a whole new language.

Powerless. Steps. Trudge. Amends. Inventory. Word after word I'd never heard before. Were they in the dictionary? "Check it out," said my sponsor. Sponsor? Another new word.

But the biggest new word of all was gratitude. Gratitude? What's that? I had never been grateful for anything in my life. I either got my due or I worked for it. There was nothing to be grateful for. I could do happy, sometimes, sort of. This, I learned, was a start. What would made me happy? Ah. Gratitude.

Gratitude, I learned, tends to multiply and grow. I found gratitude in being sober. Being sober gave me more things to be grateful for. That gratitude brought still more things to be grateful for. Oh, that wonderful pink cloud.

AA is noted for witty and wise sayings. One of my favorites is, "How do you stay sober? You don't drink and you don't die." How true that is. But in doing that, life goes on. You get old. Friends and activities and things you cherish change. Some end.

I was 48 years old when I came to AA. I'm now 80. My wife and I had to move cross-country for an affordable place to live in retirement. That left far behind all those irreplaceable AA friends and memories. Medical problems arose and deepened. During all this, my gratitude often became an exercise in day-to-day endurance. I didn't drink, but that persistent "committee" in my head started making suggestions again, such as: It wasn't that bad, was it? A little nip would sure cut down the pain.

And then the COVID pandemic came along, and my home group moved onto computers and my AA involvement went flat. I became a grumpy senior, not especially grateful for anything, even though I was just awash in things for which to be grateful. I couldn't see the big, good stuff for the small, bad stuff. Boy, did I need a solution.

The solution, I finally found, is what I call "FGG," short for fine-grain gratitude. FGG recognizes that there's always something to be grateful for. This is not in-spite-of gratitude. That's important. In-spite-of gratitude gives time and attention to the things I'm not grateful for. They don't need my attention.

If I'm flat on my back, waiting for the meds I need to take to kick in, I can instead be grateful that I have a bed to lie in and meds to take. I can be grateful for the doctor's care and the pharmacy that filled my prescription. If I'm out of my favorite breakfast cereal, I can be grateful that there's something else to eat. And so on.

This practice changes my focus from what I lack to what I have. Once I start doing that, everything changes for the better.

I'm still an occasionally grumpy senior. Pink clouds are far behind me now. I'm doing more trudging on the Road of Happy Destiny than skipping up it. But what I do know for sure—I'm sober and my cup runneth over.

Al L.
Hendersonville, North Carolina

CHAPTER FIVE

A Place We Can Call Home

Joining a home group, belonging, helping out—a place to recover that you love

The drinking life is filled with uncertainties. The sober life can be too. This makes the consistency and love we find in a home group so powerfully important to us. "I'm not an outgoing guy and I don't make friends easily," writes a member in "Happy to See My Friends." But when he walks into his 7:30 A.M. home group, he is extraordinarily grateful for the men and women he gets to share valuable time with.

Those low-ceilinged church basements that turn into sanctuaries of sobriety stir an everyday form of gratitude in many of us. We are grateful for the routine of a home group, for the coffee, for the laughter, for seeing ourselves in those around us.

Even though he is serving 30 years to life in a maximum security prison, Michael T. in "The Sweet Smell of Coffee" is grateful for the gift of sobriety he finds through the fellowship of his home group. "Each and every hour, day, month and year that I don't pick up that first drink," he writes, "I earn that gift."

Where Attraction Happens

June 2025

I hit the lottery when I found my home group. The love, care, strength and support I get there is beyond measure. We are an eclectic group—the young psychologist with a doctorate degree, the fire chief, the retired military officer, the convicted felon who spent more than 10 years away and still has an ankle bracelet. We also have city employees and self-made tradesmen among our lot. As it's been said, we would not normally mix. But we do.

The gut-wrenching honesty that comes to the surface during our meetings is invaluable. The Fellowship gives me what I need, no matter how difficult a day it was. We share each other's pain. The parent of a child struggling with addiction, the adult children who refuse to have contact, the hardships that come with living with mental and emotional disorders. It's all brought to the surface, either during the meeting or in conversations before or after.

I've picked up some great lines of wisdom here, such as, "I can afford to change this," and, "Leave room for optimism." I never know when and from whom these insights will come. And rarely does a meeting end without someone speaking about the booze.

My home group offers a lot of hope. One night a member shared that he had wanted to kill himself. A half hour later, at our group's business meeting, he was elected chair of the group. The member got through his struggles and has been doing a wonderful job in his elected position.

Our AA meeting is held at a sober clubhouse where we always see new faces. We love to celebrate someone getting their first 24 hours or just arriving from rehab. Our enthusiasm is infectious. It's wonderful to watch these new members come in and say yes to this lifesaving program.

It's been said that money can't buy happiness. No amount of money is worth more than the love, strength and support my home group gives me. It's the attraction that keeps me coming back.

Pat R.
Philadelphia, Pennsylvania

Firepit Fanatics

April 2025

"Welcome to the FFFF meeting of Alcoholics Anonymous." This is how we opened our Fabulous Friday Firepit Fanatics meeting of AA. Every week at 6:30 P.M. we meet in my semi-rural Oregon driveway, with a metal firepit blazing away.

FFFF was born in the pandemic. What an incredible blessing we forged from the lack of meetings because of all the lockdowns. In late March of 2020 when meetings were dropping like flies and virtual meetings were emergent, a handful of hearty souls and I opted for an in-person, outdoor meeting in my driveway. The core of our new meeting originally came from our Wednesday evening Grapevine study meeting, "Fearless and Thorough."

Here in Oregon, we get wet. It's part of our lifestyle. But how was it that for the longest time, Friday nights always seemed to be dry between the hours of 6:30 and 7:30? Seriously. In the 35 months of our existence, we were forced into my spacious garage only five or six times. One evening our meeting even carried on in a light, steady rain with umbrellas, hoods and jackets—and we all just laughed.

Our meeting quickly became a hardcore favorite of some who got there early to stack, set and light the fire. "It's the highlight of my week," said one member. "This meeting sets up my weekend perfectly," said another. "I like smelling like a campfire," revealed another. Sometimes the fire had an attitude and spit embers at members. We had to be on guard at all times! Other times the blaze was calmer, hot and visually mesmerizing. But every meeting was different and special and was a safe and profound space in which to go deep. No matter the topic, there always seemed to be a depth to the shares.

Like any other meeting, we gave chips, and our Seventh Tradition went to GSO in New York City. We weren't on any official schedules, so the meeting was word of mouth. Anywhere from 10 to 16 people would usually show up. Some nights some of us played music afterward in the garage. Some nights we barbecued food and had potluck fellowship. Mostly we marveled at how cool the vibe was. Dogs were welcomed and the Christmas lights were lit to celebrate and mark our meetings as a very special night.

Christmas Eve of 2022, I got sick with COVID, so I stayed inside on my couch. Outside at 6:30 in 29 degree temperature, six hearty souls had an AA meeting with a most excellent fire. Hardcore? Absolutely. Committed? Without a doubt. A little nuts? You bet. Would I trade these people for anything? No way in the world. I love these people, the fellowship, the laughing, the crying, the weather, the solidarity, the sobriety and the deep places we go to heal and help each other.

So—to Scott, Ron, Scott, Peggy, Mark, Marc, Mark, Julie, Christine, Christine, Jesse, Andrew, Andrew, Hat Tom, Chris, Martin, Elizabeth, Vanessa, Austin, Dennis, Steve and many others—I salute you. I love you and honor you all. What a meeting.

Hamish C.
Tualatin, Oregon

Happy to See My Friends
February 2025

Today I woke up when the alarm went off and hit the snooze button. The alarm woke me up again, so I hit the snooze again. It woke me up a third time! Now I had to make a decision. Do I hurry to my 7:30 A.M. AA meeting, or do my morning routine at home and catch the later meeting at 9:00? A meeting's a meeting, right? Oh, no—my 7:30 Saturday morning meeting is my anchor.

When I started coming to my 7:30 meeting there were only a few people there, sometimes less than 10. Now there are at least 20 to 30 people every week. Some regulars have more than 20 years of sobriety. There are some who I got to see in their first weeks of sobriety who now have two to three years sober and are sponsoring others. There are a couple of folks who have gone in and out. It always feels so good to see them come back and be with us.

I could meditate later, I thought. This meeting is happening now. Sobriety comes first. Nothing else is possible if I don't stay sober. So I got up and did the minimum to get myself presentable and headed off to the clubhouse. On the way I got to thinking about the Third Step, turning my will and my life over to the care of God—her plan, not mine.

Most Saturdays, no matter how I plan it, I always seem to walk in just as the meeting starts, or maybe a couple minutes after. Today traffic was light, and I actually showed up 15 minutes early. There was a crew sitting out on the front porch. I've heard most of these folks share many times. I know them well. They've heard me share. They know me too.

Inside there were five or six lively conversations going on. The woman who often leads the meeting with over 30 years of sobriety was talking with the New Age hippie lady with the long white hair. The young Asian mother of two small children was sitting with the little old woman who used to preside over a house full of her husband's musician friends. And nearby was the urban gardener lady I used to see regularly at one of the town's primo music dive bars, before either of us made it to AA.

Since I got to the meeting early, I took one of the more comfortable seats on a couch by the wall. In the chair next to me was the gay bartender who'd spent much of his life in New York City. He's almost as old as I am. We had a good laugh about 18-inch bellbottoms. And on the other side of me was a young woman who'd been having a rough couple of years but had now strung together several months sober. She had been through the punk rock thing, and she and this old guy were chatting about that.

Our meeting truly is a batch of folks who would not ordinarily mix. But we share a disease and a recovery plan, and we know some of the most honest and personal parts of one anothers' stories. We feel each others' ups and downs.

The last-minute members came in, the noise settled down and our meeting started. One of us read "On Awakening" from the Big Book, others read today's page from *Daily Reflections*. A few more stragglers came in.

I'm not an outgoing guy, and I don't make friends easily, but I looked around the room today and realized I knew all these people by name: Jose, Katherine, Jim, Jim C., Jeffery, Swan, Marcella, Cheryl, Joanie, Anna, Karen, Karenmarie, Tommy, Jeff, Ryan, Sammy, Julie, Debbie, Elva, Kevin, Roxie, Patty, Jason, Kenny, Neal, Jeff and Hard-headed Ernest. And there was another dozen familiar faces: cops, jailbirds, professionals, housewives, truck-drivers, lawyers, construction workers, chefs, all ranging in age from their 20s to their 70s.

I was reminded of the song, "Feelin' Good Again." It's about a guy coming home from a trip late at night, walking into his hometown bar, seeing friends he'd missed and feeling good again. I get that same feeling in my 7:30 AA meeting. Not every one of these friends is here every week, so I get a special feeling for each one when I see them. And it's better than any gathering I can remember.

Anonymous
Houston, Texas

Finally Home

April 2020

I love my home group and invite everyone to come visit. I'd like to think it's the best group in all AA, yet it's just a group like any other. I just happen to feel at home here. It meets every Tuesday and Thursday at a YMCA. I've come to count on it being here. The first thing I noticed about my group was how bright and cheery it is and that there's a lot of sobriety in the room.

It took me time to get to know people. I learned slowly that there were a lot of LGBTQ+ people there who had known each other for years. Some had been sober for 50 years.

I'm a transgender member, and the group embraced me very early on in my recovery. I was so shaky then. I was constantly relapsing, and the group just loved me. They listened to me and made me a part of the group. They kept electing me to service commitments, and no one batted an eye each time I picked up a drink and could no longer do the job. I have since been able to make amends to the group, living and direct, by staying sober and showing up for each commitment they put me up for now.

My entire first year, I sat next to an old gentle giant. I hid in his looming shadow. Such a sweet gentle man he was. After he passed away, I found out that he was a cofounder of our home group, which began a long time ago. I got to attend his memorial. It had such an impact on me to walk in and see my entire home group all dressed up, paying their respects.

Later, I remember getting to sign our group's lease when I was overall chair, still not entirely believing I would be able to stay sober for another entire year.

I'll never forget my first qualification in front of the group. I got weepy and was so moved. These members had watched each other get married, get jobs, lose jobs and loved ones. And they just kept coming and loving one another. All I've ever wanted is to love and be loved in return and to grow old with somebody. Here before my eyes, I could see my home group doing just that with one another.

When I mentioned that they were growing old together, the entire room gasped. Did I really just call them old? How funny. I guess I did! It was such a special moment.

Oh well ... I guess I'll keep coming back. They have what I want.

L.M.
Brooklyn, New York

Letters From Home

July 2024

The support of my home group has been a crucial part of my recovery. I generally attend meetings with this group four or five times a week. Identifying one group as my home group helps keep me accountable while allowing me to be vulnerable and transparent by sharing openly with friends I know well. I've found that to heal and recover from my alcoholism, I need to let others into my world. When I was drinking, I isolated a lot. Today, to achieve some level of emotional sobriety, I need the help of other recovering alcoholics. I can't do this alone.

Just after my first AA birthday, I was facing charges from an old DUI which resulted in me going to jail. During the months leading up to my incarceration, I relied heavily on the support of my home group. I learned early on that I needed to have relationships with other members, so when a crisis occurred, I'd have an established support system. I thank God that was one suggestion I followed through on.

On the morning of my sentencing, I arrived at the courthouse, and to my surprise there were five or six members from my home group there to support me. Their hugs and words of encouragement meant the world to me. As the judge sentenced me and I was led away in handcuffs, I knew I was not alone. Not only did I know that my Higher Power was with me, but my home group was there as well.

During the time I was incarcerated, I received a steady stream of cards and letters, all from members of my home group. Rarely did a day go by when I did not receive at least one piece of mail. This took place during the COVID pandemic, so I was locked in my cell along with my three cellmates for 23 hours every day.

One day two of my cellmates were whispering to each other. Finally one of them looked over at me and asked, "Who are you?" I thought this was odd because by this time we all knew each others' names, but I told them my name anyway. They then said, "No, who are you really?" Only then did I realize they were referring to the amount of mail I was receiving. They thought I was a celebrity and that was all my fan mail!

Members of my home group saw to it that I had a Big Book, a copy of *Twelve Steps and Twelve Traditions* and *Daily Reflections*, and of course, the latest issue of Grapevine. All this encouragement and support made my time in jail much more tolerable. With the literature they sent me, I was able to share some AA with my cellmates. They especially liked reading the stories in Grapevine and in the back of the Big Book.

Every day I felt the love and support of my dear AA friends. Now that's the power of a home group.

Suzanne A.
Dalton, Georgia

Best Cake & Coffee Going

From: ***Dear Grapevine***
May 2020

I have the best home group ever. My group is everything that everyone talks about. We even provide childcare to those who have a difficult time getting to meetings. Our "meetings before the meeting" are always warm, often with intense conversations. We laugh together, cry together and course have the best cake and coffee going.

There are a few of us who pray and meditate in the sanctuary, which enhances our individual spiritual paths. We love each other even more when life seems to be heavy on the heart and soul. I have found my unity, service and recovery here.

What more could anyone want from their home group?

Irving M.
Washington, D.C.

The Sweet Smell of Coffee

April 2020

I arrived at the maximum-security state prison at Elmira, N.Y. in 2014. As the correctional bus pulled up to the facility, I could never have imagined beyond my wildest dreams what I'd discover up on that hill.

The prison building's structure has an intimidating appearance, with a really high wall. It's got to be at least 40 feet high. Once inside the facility, I was soon greeted by an inmate who asked me if I was interested in attending AA there. I was open to the suggestion. I had been in and out of trouble and in and out of solitary confinement. My life was pretty unmanageable.

I will always remember my first AA meeting here at Elmira. I was quite nervous. The group was called The Hill Group and it was held in the facility's school building. This one was on a Wednesday night, and I was told ahead of time that there'd be outside AA members in attendance.

I had always struggled in social settings when alcohol wasn't involved. And I was an introvert. But whatever anxiety I experienced that night subsided. I received a warm welcome by everyone at the meeting. Moreover, I had the opportunity to meet at least 20 different sober prisoners who lived in various housing units throughout the complex.

What I definitely remember is the smell of coffee brewing. The room was decorated with all these AA slogans, and there was plenty of literature—tons of it. I welcomed myself to some literature. I learned about the history of The Hill Group. It's been in existence since President Kennedy was in the White House! Also, this group has saved many, many lives of inside members, as well as outside members.

During the meeting, we went around the room reading the Preamble, the Steps and some AA literature. The chairperson that night stressed the importance of anonymity and asked if there were any newcomers, so I raised my hand. Later, we had a coffee break and when the meeting ended, we gathered and said the Lord's Prayer. They told me to come back. I'm glad I did.

At one point in my life, I wanted the world and everything in it. Unfortunately, alcohol and other substances had their way with me. I came to prison for the first time at the age of 31. I now had a sentence of 30 years to life.

I truly believe that The Hill Group has made me a better person. Prison is full of negativity and temptations. Every day above water is a good day in here. I've learned that alcoholism is a disease that strikes at random; it doesn't discriminate. When I sit in my group here and look around the room, I see guys from every conceivable walk of life. When I listen to other members share their stories, I feel something deep down inside myself. I learn that other people are no better nor less than me. We're all equal in AA regardless of how much sobriety we may or may not have.

Our elections for service at The Hill Group are coming up. I've held the literature position for the past year. It was such a rewarding experience. However, I can't say that I've read all the literature yet. I will say that what I read has made me more knowledgeable about the history of AA, how it started and why it still exists today.

Before I found AA in prison, I was labeled by the administration as a disruptive inmate. Convicts who know me can attest to that. Finding this group is saving my rear each and every day. Growing up and taking responsibility for my actions, past and present, is what I do today. It's who I am. My relationships with family and friends have improved dramatically since joining AA. Now it's about working the Steps, carrying the message and improving my relationship with my Higher Power.

I started a hobby in here about a year ago, painting subjects in different mediums. A fellow member at our group was kind enough to give me some of his extra paint brushes. This took my imagination to new levels. Recently, with help from various family members, I was able to turn my cell into a little art studio. I've painted several pieces since and sent them to family and friends for the holidays. The feedback from everyone has been overwhelming. I owe that to The Hill Group.

I've been incarcerated almost 17 years now. I may never see the outside world again. I have good days and bad ones. But don't we all? I know I must continue to change.

For me, sobriety is a gift that's earned every single day, just like most people earn a living on the outside world. Each and every hour, day, month and year that I don't pick up that first drink, I earn that gift. And then I try to help another member achieve that same reward.

Michael T.
Stormville, New York

CHAPTER SIX

Doing Our Part—Helping Others

One of the great gifts of doing service is what you get back in return

Being of service for the sake of service is the most heartfelt expression of gratitude that we can offer. As Bill W. wrote in our AA literature, we strive "to be humbly grateful and exert ourselves in a spirit of love and service." This chapter expresses that beautifully.

In Lea V.'s story "In Service of Service," she describes overcoming her shyness and being led to get involved by a sponsor, little by little, until in the end she is "grateful for the willingness to walk through fear and be of service."

Quite often we work for AA anonymously, as Connor D. writes in "Doing My Part." Tradition Twelve, he writes, "teaches me to be a trusted servant, regardless of any recognition or merit. ... I hope I can make the best cup of coffee possible for the next newcomer who walks through our doors. They may not remember my face. They may not remember my name. But maybe they'll remember that warm cup of coffee."

Coffee Queen

May 2020

During my first year of sobriety, I got the best ever service job in all of AA. I got to pour coffee at Chicago's Irving Park YMCA for the Sunday morning breakfast speaker meeting. More than 100 people attended each week, and I must say that it was the first time I realized how many people were sober in AA outside my home group and the other three meetings a week I attended.

I was a little nervous at first. I had to fill the small coffeepot at the big cauldron in the enormous kitchen and carefully carry it to the long tables in the dining room. I very gingerly walked behind all the chairs, reaching around the members and carefully pouring the scalding hot coffee, praying I wouldn't get an attack of the jitters.

After a couple of weeks of service, I was starting to feel like an old hand and was really enjoying the job. I found that I had The Power of the Pot. When I'm in charge of pouring coffee elixir to AA members on a Sunday morning, I am the Coffee Queen!

In very short order, everyone knew my name! I'd hear people calling, "Hey Carol, over here, please." I felt like I was in that sitcom based in a bar where everybody knows your name. I learned to smile all the time, to say thank you dozens of times each morning.

It made me feel really good about myself for the first time in a very long time. A big bonus was meeting members from all over our area, although I didn't know at that time that Chicago was its own area and the YMCA was part of the northwest Chicago district in which I lived.

There were other bonuses. I really learned how to listen and to identify with the speaker no matter how little our stories matched. I remember when I heard a most outrageous story of a fellow's family enabling him almost to death and I was thinking that there was no way I could get anything out of his talk. Then he ended his story by saying that he came into AA after he called his family yet one more time to ask for help. His mother answered the phone. He said, "Hi, it's John," and she said, "John who?" I got the speaker's point right away, as my family had been at the point of not picking up my calls either.

I also heard a story from a former nun who had some hair-raising adventures. She got nicknamed "The Flying Nun" after a popular TV show at the time because after a few nips during the school day, she went out on the playground with the kids and put all her students on the merry-go-round, pushed it faster and faster, her habit flying in the wind, and then jumped on, drunk and laughing. Again, I was wondering what I could learn from her story. That's when it hit me. She spoke of the shame, the guilt, the regret, the humiliation, and I thought, Yes, that was me to a T.

The best lesson I heard was while I was seated one morning just as the meeting started and someone was reading "How It Works." I had the most important thing to say to a friend across the table. As I leaned across, ignoring the person reading, I whispered my news loudly to my friend. Then I felt an elbow jab into my ribs, taking my breath away. I turned to see that Katie, who sat next to me almost every Sunday morning, had elbowed me. She had always been so friendly to me from my very earliest meetings and I looked up to her as a mentor. I raised my eyebrows, questioning. She leaned over to hiss in my ear, "What's the matter? Don't you need to hear this anymore?"

I was mortified. I told myself that I would never speak to her again as I listened to the rest of the meeting. But I got over my hurt feelings, and believe me when I tell you, I never talked through a reading at a meeting again. I had learned a painful lesson.

I'm forever grateful to the AA members at the YMCA every Sunday morning who let me pour their coffee and loved me enough to put me on a good sobriety track. Service is the glue that keeps me in the AA seat.

Carol K.
Sarasota, Florida

Maximum Picnic

July 2018

Six years ago, I found myself in the parking lot outside of what would be my first AA meeting. Just released from jail, I was terrified and angry. Why had I listened to that guy from the AA helpline? I didn't want to be here. I may have just been released from jail but I felt sure my life wasn't that unmanageable. Or was it?

I'd rather be dead than go into the meeting, but I had reached a state of hopelessness that I never imagined I would sink to. And yet, with a gentle shove from God, I moved slowly toward the door. I saw a man standing in the entrance with his back turned to me. I approached him and asked if this was AA. He turned around and gave me a big smile. "Yes, it is," he said. "I am so glad you made it here. We've been waiting for you."

So, full of shame and guilt, I walked down those stairs and took a seat. I was amazed at how many people were there. With the ring of a bell, the man who greeted me at the door began to speak. The room fell silent. I don't remember much about what was said, but I do remember the topic of discussion. It was Step One.

Looking back now, I feel God had handpicked each member there that night. I heard myself in every one of those members who shared their stories. I knew I was in the right place. I was home.

Just two nights earlier, I had woken up in a different jail cell. I swore it would never happen again, yet there I was again. And this time it was the worst. I called out to God. It was the first time I earnestly did that. I truly believe he answered my desperate plea.

Covered in blood, without my shoes and still in my pajamas from a few days earlier, I was confused and full of remorse and dread. I was taken from my cell, after sleeping off the worst of it, and led down a seemingly endless hallway where I was fingerprinted and photographed.

I began to remember small bits of what had happened. My stomach sank as I recalled my son's screams for help after I wrecked my car. Fortunately, the impact had been on my side. I found my car wrapped around a utility pole. If things had gone differently, I could have killed my son. For me, the end had arrived. Either I got help or I died.

Hours passed. I was finally released with a promise to appear in court. I was now facing serious charges and if I were convicted, I could serve many years behind bars. Truth was, I already felt like I was in a kind of prison.

Someone then put me in the back seat of a taxicab, still without shoes, covered in blood and not knowing where my son was. To be honest, I never even asked. I was driven home, jail papers in hand, where I would break into my parents' house, steal more of their money to pay the cab driver, and invite him in for a drink. He swiftly declined the offer and I slammed the door in his face.

I knew a drink would make it all disappear. Even after my plea to God and my desperate call for help, I still wanted a drink. Then oblivion came.

The following day, I made a call to AA, a call that would forever change my life. I have remained sober ever since. AA showed me that what I thought was impossible—a life without booze—was possible.

After I'd been sober about four months, I was approached by a member to attend a meeting at a prison. I thought it was a joke at first. I had been locked up in that very prison. I never thought I'd ever go back there, especially for an AA meeting! Reluctantly, I agreed. AA had never said no to me, so how could I say no to AA?

That Friday night, I sat with incarcerated AA members for the very first time. I was still new then, still angry and full of fear. Then a member said, "Ruth, why don't you share how you have stayed sober." That prison meeting was a life-changing experience for me. I saw myself in every member sitting there. I could have easily been any one of them. From that moment on, attending prison meetings has remained a privilege and an honor. We have all done bad things; that doesn't make us bad people. Today, some of my favorite people call prison their home.

Not long ago, I was invited to attend an AA picnic at a "supermax" prison in upstate New York. I had visited this institution a few times before and was grateful to be invited to join our friends for this annual event. But I had no idea what a prison picnic would be like.

When we arrived at the facility, we were escorted by guards and began the long walk down the empty hallways, stopping frequently for more security checks. Passing the separated yards through the heavily barred windows, I caught a small glimpse of the lives living there. Shivers went up my spine. I felt overwhelmed as my eyes began to fill. I had a giant lump in my throat. I got to see for the first time how these men live every single day. Endless towering concrete walls as high as the sky, razor wire and fences everywhere. Guards everywhere. I was deafened by the silence. It was like entering another world. I was sad, yet happy and excited. I was feeling so many things all at once that I thought I'd burst. In that moment, I paused and reached out to God.

When we finally reached our yard, we were led by the guards and filed in one by one. Word was sent out to another group of guards to send in the inmates. The outside AA members had arrived.

The sober inmates had been busy preparing for this day. A group of picnic tables had been assembled under a giant canopy to shelter us from the sun. Tables for food were set up and ready. There was even a DJ table for music. But where are the guys? I thought. Why is it taking so long? Then, out of the corner of my eye I saw a shadow. I turned quickly to see who was there but whatever had been there was gone. I looked across the yard and goose bumps covered my body. I felt the presence of God. I took a silent moment and asked him to bring us all together.

Just then, the men walked into the yard. The sun was shining and they were all smiling. The joy and freedom I saw in their eyes was magical. With a silent nod and warm handshake, we all stood together. For a moment, it seemed we all forgot where we were. The razor wire disappeared; the giant walls no longer seemed so towering. We talked one-to-one and in small groups. Like at any other meeting, we shared together, caught up and then made our way to the canopy. The AA meeting in the yard was about to begin. I began to cry.

The prisoners led the AA meeting. I was filled with such gratitude listening to our friends share. It was something I will never forget.

In the yard of a supermax prison, I heard hope, I saw love and I felt at home. It was amazing. I witnessed as grown men cried and laughed together. These men were my friends.

Since the picnic was an annual gathering, we were given much more time with the guys. We sat and had lunch that the sober inmates had prepared for us. Afterward, we listened to music and talked and talked. The day gave me so much joy. It was like nothing I have ever experienced.

As members of AA, we are given such amazing opportunities to serve. I now know what it means to be of maximum service to the Fellowship that saved my life.

When the picnic ended, we were allowed to gather together for a group photo, for those who wished to join. On the count of three, several pictures were taken, one of which now sits in a frame on my bedside table as a lasting memory. I keep it close to my heart. Every day, I wake up to my beautiful friends' faces and give thanks to AA and God.

Ruth L.
Beaconsfield, Quebec

Inside Raymondville

December 2020

Recently, at an AA meeting in my area, I happened to see the Grapevine annual prison issue (July 2018), with the headline: "Free on the Inside." Wow, those words brought forth a lot of old memories and increased my gratitude once again.

My husband and I used to travel from Canada to southern Texas for the winter months from 2003 until his death in 2016. I've gone there myself a couple of times since he passed. I found that there is an amazing AA community in that part of Texas.

In December 2010, I was sitting at a district meeting in the South Padre Island/Port Isabel area, where I heard a speaker named David say that members were needed to help bring AA meetings into Willacy Prison in Raymondville.

I felt that God was touching my heart and saying in no uncertain terms that I needed to help out. I went up and asked the speaker if he thought a woman from Canada would be able to help. "Let's find out," he replied.

It turned out, yes, indeed I'd be able to participate. Before long, a few of us drove off together for Gatesville, Texas, to do our official prison training. A short time later, I started helping out with that prison meeting, which was called "Free on the Inside."

The drive from South Padre Island to Raymondville is an hour and a half long. We had some great "meetings" before and after the AA meeting, on the road to and from the prison.

Each week, about 50 prisoners attended the meeting. During the week of Christmas, we got permission to bring food into the prison for a special celebration. We stopped on our way and got milk and various sodas, as well as all kinds of delicious Mexican pastries. The milk seemed to be their favorite of the treats.

Without exception, each week the men thanked us a lot. Some even said, "God bless you" when we were leaving. The prison chaplain told us that he saw a big difference in the men's attitudes and participation at the other regular prison activities after they attended their AA meetings.

One of the biggest impacts of doing this kind of service for me was an increase in my own gratitude. That gratitude began with the sound of the gates clanging shut behind us as we went inside and again after we left. That clanging when we were outside again was my own special "free on the outside" feeling.

I will always be grateful for those years in Raymondville.

Helaine D.
Sudbury, Ontario

It Keeps Getting Better

September 2025

I'm celebrating five years of sobriety this month, and I can tell you they have been the best five years of my life, bar none. Not only has my journey been miraculous, but I've gotten to help others get sober too.

Recently my wife Darlene found a letter I had written to her back when I was still drinking. I had been sleeping in the basement for the third time in our 25-year marriage. I was in trouble and didn't think I could fast-talk my way back again. So I wrote her a letter telling her why I was a great husband. Here's the list.

1) I have an excellent job.
2) I have provided a great house to live in with a double garage and two nice cars.
3) I'm an amazing athlete in great shape.
4) I'm a wonderful father.
5) I have lots of friends who love spending time with us.
6) I'm not a gambler.
7) I'm not an alcoholic or drug user.
8) I don't fool around with other women.
9) I control my anger.
10) I'm a very loving and great lover.

Holy egomaniac! This letter was my attempt at keeping our marriage together. I told my wife, "Something has to change."

"That's right," Darlene said. "You have to change." I knew she was right, and I knew what I had to do. My brother had been in AA for seven years, and over that time I saw a huge change in him. I searched online and went to my first AA meeting. That was five years ago.

The first fellow I met in AA was Reuben. I told him, "I don't know what to do." He said, "Just keep an open mind and wait for the miracle to happen." I listened to everyone sharing their stories and thought I might be an alcoholic. But there was a lot of "God talk" and mentions of Higher Powers, and the meeting closed with the Lord's Prayer with everyone holding hands. I left quickly, thinking this was a religious program and not for me.

When I got home, my wife asked me how it went. I said there were some people with stories like mine, but "I think it's a religious program." She looked at me with tears in her eyes and said, "Are you going back?" I wanted to say, "Not a chance," but I'm a sucker for a woman crying and replied, "Of course, honey, they said to keep coming back." So went to 90 meetings in 90 days, got a sponsor—Dave M., who had what I wanted—and he took me through the Steps.

After the first two weeks, I could say I was an alcoholic, and after the first month I had my first spiritual moment when I broke down crying while sharing in the meeting. Everyone told me how amazing it was. I still hear about that share five years later.

At my one-year celebration, I told my sponsor Dave that I didn't think this sober life could get any better. He told me to sponsor someone, and my second year got even better. After two years, I told Dave "My life can't get better than this," and he said, "Host a Step meeting at your home." So I did, and it got even better. Then after three years—and in the middle of the COVID pandemic when we only had online meetings—I said, "Well, Dave, how can it get any better?" Dave told me I should start having outside meetings behind the church. So I did, and people came from everywhere, practicing social distancing and wearing masks.

At year four I once again told Dave it couldn't possibly get any better. He said "Now that the group is back inside the church, start running daily meetings." So I did, and people once again came out in record numbers. Our home group went from about eight members to almost 50 today. Here I am, celebrating my fifth year in AA this month. Now when I look back at my old list of why I was such a great husband, I just laugh. What an egotistical, self-centered jerk I was!

After five years, getting some humility and service under my belt, sponsoring several men, doing the Steps a number of times and learning to love my fellow alcoholics in a way I never thought possible, I have revised my list. Here's why I'm a grateful alcoholic and husband today:

1) I have learned to work together with others at my job.
2) We have a loving, caring home environment and live in peace.
3) I'm a team player in sports and try my best and help other players be team players.
4) I try to be a caring father, and I think it's working because every year our kids tell me they love their new dad even more.
5) My old friends are still OK and like the changes in me, but my new AA friends have shown me what true love really is.
6) I'm still not a gambler. Yea!
7) I am a recovered alcoholic.
8) I'm a dedicated husband and friend to the beautiful woman I married who recently said, "I always knew deep down that you were the man you have become."
9) I listen patiently and get angry very rarely, as I try to strive for progress, not perfection.
10) I try to be an empathetic, loving partner.

So, Dave, "How can this get any better?"

Paul K.
Burlington, Ontario

In Service of Service

Grapevine Online Exclusive
May 2024

My first sponsor instilled being of service within my first week of sobriety. She had me putting books away or washing coffee cups. In a couple of months, I had a coffee position. Then at six months I stood for a secretary position. I learned early that on having a responsibility to the group helps keep me sober and allows me to give back to Alcoholics Anonymous.

I continued this type of service for the next two years. At just over a year, I had finished the Steps and at about a year and a half I knew it was time to get uncomfortable and switch sponsors. I also knew that it was time to challenge myself with my next service commitment and ultimately stood for and was elected our group's General Service Representative.

I started my GSR commitment and met new people at District meetings and Area Assemblies. Slowly, I learned what my service commitment meant and really started to enjoy being of service at that level. The friends I met in my new position allowed me to expand my circle. The first time I had to travel as GSR was to Kona for the Budget Assembly, where I wound up staying in the home of a wonderful woman and her family. I felt welcomed and comfortable and enjoyed meeting new people in each of the island's area assemblies.

I never thought I would be so grateful for the willingness to walk through the fear and be of service as a GSR. I have opened my home to others who are being of service and now have friendships that will last a lifetime. Not only that, but I have found a way to do my part in making sure Alcoholics Anonymous is around for generations to come.

Lea V.
Kula, Maui, Hawaii

Family Affair

From: *Dear Grapevine*
January 2017

My father was once a GSR for his home group back in Guadalajara, Mexico. I thought a GSR was like a manager of the group or something. Service is one of the best things my father passed on to our family.

After he passed away, my mother and my oldest brother told me how happy he was that I was not drinking anymore. After 10 years in the program, I too got involved in general service. Today I have 30 years and my wife, daughter and son are all part of my AA family.

I never thought that being sober would bring me so many beautiful things. In 2008, my district sent me to Alaska for PRAASA, and when I came back to report, I could not hide my feelings because it put so much joy in my heart. General service has taken me to places that I've never been before. I had the privilege to serve as an area officer and I'm currently serving as a panel 65 delegate for my area. Now that's God doing for me what I cannot do for myself.

Raymundo L.
San Jose, California

Saying Yes

From: ***Dear Grapevine***
January 2016

When I was little, my dad used to always say, "Shari, you're too sensitive!" Because of my self-centeredness, I was so hyper-aware of myself. Turns out that was a character defect.

For me, a big part of doing service in AA is being willing to stand up, make a mistake and accept criticism. If I hide in the rooms, if I don't raise my hand to share, if I don't tell my story, if I don't sponsor and if I don't do coffee or chair meetings or do service for the district or area, then I stay "safe" in AA. There are no opportunities to make a mistake and my sensitive ego stays protected.

So in order to be of maximum service to those about me, I have to be willing to stand up, to say yes, to take a risk and put myself out there. So far it has paid off enormously! I offer a genuine thank you to all members who are willing to say yes when AA needs us to help.

Shari M.
Clarkston, Virginia

Doing My Part

May 2024

When I first walked into the rooms of AA, everything was ready. The meeting lists were made available by the local intergroup, the doors were open, the lights were on, the literature was out on the table, the message was shared by members and the coffee was brewing.

There wasn't a thing I had to do. No dues or fees to pay. I could just walk in. They had everything I needed, especially the coffee. And boy, did I drink it. I don't remember who made the coffee. I really can't remember their faces or their names. I do, however, remember drinking cup after cup as if my life depended on it.

My entrance into AA makes me think about our Twelfth Tradition, which states that, "Anonymity is the spiritual foundation of all our traditions, ever reminding us to place principles before personalities." Today I understand that this Tradition teaches me to be a trusted servant, regardless of any recognition or merit. I don't seek validation for doing acts of service, lest I let my ego rear its head.

Today I must keep an attitude of gratitude, completing my acts of service as if my efforts will never be known or acknowledged. I must give back what was given to me. We do our AA service. We pay the rent on our facilities, we provide the literature, and we make sure the coffee is made so that someone who hasn't yet found their bearing can just walk in and have a seat.

I hope I can make the best cup of coffee possible for the next newcomer who walks through our doors. They may not remember my face. They may not remember my name. But maybe they'll remember that warm cup of coffee.

To those who came before me and who made sure that the doors were open and the lights were on, I'd just like to say: "Thanks for the coffee!"

Connor D.
Austin, Texas

CHAPTER SEVEN

Belief & Faith

The joy of finding and connecting with something bigger than us

Gratitude for a Higher Power is a distinctive feature of sobriety, a gratitude which often goes hand in hand with the faith that we are cared for and that we are not alone, as the stories in this inspiring chapter attest.

In the story "Talking to Air," Jay M., newly and precariously sober, is working as a bartender. He starts talking to himself in order not to pick up a drink left on the bar, a practice he continues. "At times I'm engulfed with gratitude, and I feel a real spiritual connection," Jay writes. "That's when I look up and say thank you to God as I understand him."

A newcomer who had been on the verge of suicide in Kevin F.'s story "A Place in the Sun" instead discovers himself watching dolphins with his delighted 2-year-old daughter and thanking God with tears rolling down his cheeks. "I was suddenly filled with intense gratitude and light for being alive to witness the moment," he writes.

Whisper of Freedom

October 2020

I used to be a teacher and a coach. I was actually sober for two years before the legal system took my case to trial. I'm now serving a five-year sentence for a DUI. My incarceration is almost over and I should be eligible for work release soon.

I never would have guessed that I would find my personal key to freedom during long, sleepless nights surrounded by the ever-present scents of cold steel and new cement in a cell in a small town in Minnesota.

But somehow, things slowed down enough during my incarceration in here for me to reflect on what was missing in my recovery. Through the distractions of deep booming snores of a stranger sleeping just three feet above me and the dimly lit overhead light that never goes to sleep, a gentle voice appeared as a whisper in my ear as I lay on my cardboard-like pillow in the steel bunk that I've come to accept as my bed.

That night, I distinctly heard this voice softly, but very clearly, telling me, "Rest, my son. You've finally found me. I can see your heart. I believe in you. Trust in the willingness you're feeling. I see you. I'm with you. Trust your new faith. You're finally getting honest with yourself and with me. I am pleased. I will lead you on a better path."

That seems like a lot to hear from a whisper at 2 A.M. inside a six by nine prison cell. I couldn't believe it was happening myself. But since that night, I've continued praying about those words that were whispered to me. I've become more willing to go even further in faith by being honest and taking action, such as stepping aside when my ego and perfectionism arise. I pray to this voice—which I call Papa, my Higher Power—to lead me. And I ask for the willingness to follow and the ability to watch his will for me flourish from the inside out.

I don't know if this is what AA calls a spiritual awakening, but I know that I was not asleep when I heard him. Each day now, my eyes are led to amazing insights in the pages of *Daily Reflections*, *As Bill Sees It* and our Big Book. I have even begun to write honest, resentment-free amends letters inside my prison cell as I live in this newfound freedom.

I hope this essay will help someone else who's incarcerated and feeling lonely. I am now helping facilitate the prisonwide AA meeting here. We have AA volunteers who come in from Bloomington to help share their experience, strength and hope from the outside world. We meet once a week. This prison holds 2,300 souls. Our group is growing, but we could still use all the prayers we can get.

Thanks to these "whispers of freedom," the Promises of AA are finally becoming real for me, right here on my steel bunk, with a cardboard-like pillow in a cell in a small town in Minnesota.

Daniel L.
Faribault, Minnesota

I Hear the Message

May 2014

I was still drinking when I came to my first meeting. For a year and a half, I changed my sobriety date many times. By God's grace I finally got sober on December 23, 1970.

I'm not only an alcoholic, but I suffer from grave emotional and mental disorders, and because of that, God has sent teachers my way. Everyone in my home group knew that I couldn't read, but nothing was ever said. At four months of sobriety, I walked into my regular Saturday night meeting and a long-timer presented me with a brown paper bag.

I asked, "What's this?" He said, "You'll understand when you get home. And don't tell anyone what I've done." I couldn't wait to get home. I looked inside the bag and in it were 17 90-minute tapes. He had read the entire Big Book on tape for me! The following Saturday he explained, "If you are going to be successful in AA you need to know what's in that book, and now you do."

In my first year, a young couple read and taped Grapevine for me each month. After five years, an AA buddy helped me get a driver's license by reading the manual on tape for me. Since I had been in the military, another member said that I should go to the VA hospital for an evaluation, so I saw a specialist and was diagnosed as dyslexic. He also found me a teacher at the local community college who gave me private instructions to help me read better. I later became eligible for talking books, and a reading group for the blind read all my textbooks and all my AA books onto tape for me. That helped me get my GED.

At 10 years sober, my sponsor arranged for me to do service taping AA conventions. I told him that I was not capable because of my dyslexia. He said that he and three other men would set everything up and all I had to do was go and do it! Before I started, I spoke with my wife, who said she would help. My children were very young then, and the five of us started to go to AA conferences. Today, luckily, AA literature is available on tape. I also can listen to Grapevine on my smartphone, which I enjoy a lot.

When I was new in AA, a member said that if you didn't have a God that was big enough, kind enough and good enough, he would share his God with anyone who needed one. I remember saying to myself, "Yes, I'll borrow his God." It took me eight years to return his HP. I thanked him for the use of his God because I had now found my own. Thank you Higher Power for all the help these many years.

Mack Mc.
Pitcairn, Pennsylvania

Talking to Air

September 2024

Having been raised as an Irish Catholic, as well as an altar boy and a potential seminarian, I was infused early on with a solid belief in God. But when my drinking started at 14 my spiritual beliefs began to move in a new direction—to the distilled type from a bottle. Alcohol gave me a freedom much different than I felt in church. As was expected of a lad my age, I continued to attend church, but my interest was waning.

When I was 15, my father passed away. I received a lot of sympathy from friends and family during the funeral and later, but mostly I found that I was able to drink more without much criticism due to my "emotional state." Life changed dramatically. I began to drink with much more fervor and frequency. To try to keep me on the straight and narrow, my mother had me join a youth group that was faith-based, which also had a social side. Those in my age group enjoyed partying. As my drinking progressed, I started to question my spiritual life.

At 18, I joined the Navy and left home for training. One day a shore patrol officer tracked me down at an off-base apartment to tell me to report to the chaplain. The chaplain informed me that my mother had passed away and I had to go home. It was an Irish wake and funeral, so nobody noticed that I drank to oblivion and had little memory until the burial.

I quickly developed a resentment against God. Who would take two people from me that I still really needed in life? After the funeral, I was back in the Navy on my own and quickly replaced heavenly spirits with liquid spirits. I turned into that person who would argue against the existence of God at the drop of a hat. As an obnoxious alcoholic, I always felt I had to prove that I was right, which didn't exactly make me a hit at parties. With all the events going on in the world, I thought, why would anyone believe that there was a loving God?

Soon my job performance deteriorated, and I started to miss work. The Navy saw I had a problem with alcohol and transferred me to a treatment program. I was introduced to AA, but I was not ready to go to any lengths to recover. To me, "any lengths" meant God and I was not ready to embrace that. Difficulty with the "God word" would build up inside me because I wasn't willing to ask for help. That led to a 10-year journey in and out of the rooms.

At age 31 I was back to attending AA meetings regularly and had some hope, but since I was still not willing to change I drank periodically. One day when I had two days sober (again), while sitting in a room waiting for my regular men's meeting to start, the thought occurred to me that I might try something different. I asked a man to sponsor me. He required me to make that men's meeting my home group. That's when my life changed.

I still argued when someone at a meeting said the word God. I would mumble "Higher Power" under my breath. But my sponsor had me read Appendix II, "Spiritual Experience" in the back of the Big Book. One line that struck me was, "Any alcoholic capable of honestly facing his problems in the light of our experience can recover, provided he does not close his mind to all spiritual concepts. He can only be defeated by an attitude of intolerance or belligerent denial."

When I finally stopped drinking, I got a job as a bartender at a restaurant. One Sunday brunch a man came in and sat at the bar. After a while, he said he'd like to buy me a shot. I figured I could pour the drink, then he would get called for his table and I could pour it back into the bottle. But he didn't leave. The shot sat there, and I found myself growing angrier by the minute, at AA and at life in general. Though I did not recognize it at the time, what I was really trying to do was justify taking the drink. I quietly looked to the ceiling and said, "If you want me to not have the drink, you better do something." That challenge to "whatever" was as spiritual as I could be at the time.

Just then a waiter came to the bar to get a drink order. Sam was eight years sober at the time and knew that I was only sober a few months. He noticed that I was not happy and asked me what was going on. I told him that the drink had been sitting there for a while and everyone was starting to anger me. He suggested that I throw the drink in the sink and if I still felt angry, I could pour another later.

In an attempt to show him that he didn't know what the heck he was talking about, I threw the drink into the sink. The bar was so busy I had no real time to think. After a while, I took a break and noticed that my attitude had changed. It didn't occur to me until later that I had asked for help.

That week I went to my men's meeting and was discussing the event with someone before the meeting. I told him that it seemed like something happened, but to be truthful, when I asked for help, I felt like I was just talking to air.

The man I was talking to always kept things simple. He taught me his short version of the Third Step Prayer: In the morning say "help" and at night say "thanks." He knew of my difficulty with a Higher Power. After I finished making my point, he looked at me and simply said, "Then why don't you keep talking to air. It seems to be working."

My sobriety progressed with turning my will and life over to something I wasn't concerned with explaining. I went on to write my Fourth Step. It was only after my Fifth Step that I felt a connection with some spirituality. The Promises that follow the Fifth Step say, "We may have had certain spiritual beliefs, but now we begin to have a spiritual experience." That's what happened to me. My level of spirituality grew as I went through the remaining Steps and began to feel that something had been taking care of me.

I took my last drink in September of 1985. At times I'm engulfed with gratitude, and I feel a real spiritual connection. That's when I look up and say thank you to God as I understand him. However, if I'm in self-doubt or some type of minor depression, I again feel like I'm talking to air. But as my AA friend said, "It seems to be working."

Jay M.
Carlsbad, California

Glad to Be Here

September 2025

When I was first introduced to the AA program, the question I kept hearing was, "Do you want what we've got?" Naturally, I was dumbfounded by this query. Why in the world would I want what you have? You people had alcoholism. All I had were a few minor problems when I put alcohol in my system.

I don't recall the day I accepted the fact that I've got what you've got. Acknowledging that I'm an alcoholic did nothing to keep that annoying question from getting tossed around like a beach ball at a rock concert. Sure, I wanted what you had, but I believed I had an easier, softer way than how you guys were doing it.

I don't need to waste time telling you how well my bright ideas worked out. Only when I surrendered to a Higher Power and the Steps was I able to truly see what you had and begin to work toward getting it. After 43 years of sobriety, I believe in my heart and can say with confidence, "I've got what you've got"—serenity, contentment and a life that's happy, joyous and free.

The other day I took my dogs to a park near the reservoir to let them run free. They had more than 30 acres of grass and woods to romp and frolic in. There were rabbits and squirrels to chase. All kinds of fun to be had, beauty to explore, butterflies to chase. And what did they choose to do? Run straight to the biggest pile of deer poop in the park and roll around in it. Those of you who have dogs like mine know that they were having the time of their lives. No amount of pleading would get them to stop.

It occurred to me that my alcoholism led me to do the same thing. God gave me hills to hike, lakes to swim, bike trails to ride, sunsets and sunrises to enjoy. And I responded by finding the biggest pile of alcohol-infused mess and rolling around in it—then lying to myself that I was having the time of my life.

Not rolling around like that was hardly the only thing or the most important thing I needed to learn when I started to live a sober life. I had to learn how to be a friend—a friend to you and a friend to myself. I had to learn how to love others and learn that I was lovable as well. I had to be taught how to say "please" without automatically assuming you were going to say "no" because I wasn't worth your time. I had to learn how to say "thank you" without wondering what you wanted from me—because, let's face it, my alcoholic mind told me the only reason you would help me is to get something in return.

I had to learn how to take no for an answer without thinking, What? You think you're too good for me? I had to learn to celebrate the blessings others received from God without wondering why he loved them more than he loved me. I had to learn to be happy for people's successes and not snicker at their failures. Wishing bad luck on others only ensured that it would be my constant companion. I needed to learn that my successes weren't going to change the world and that my failures weren't going to end it.

I didn't know how to be an "us." I had no clue how to be a "we." I had to learn how to be part of a fellowship and contribute to unity. Fellowship, sistership, friendship and unity will let me know I'm on the right path.

Perhaps the most challenging and elusive was when I had to be taught how to laugh. I had to learn to laugh with my fellows and with my Higher Power. I had to learn that if I didn't laugh at myself, I was missing out on the best joke. For someone who was as smart as I was when I came to AA, I sure had a lot to learn.

September 18, 1979 was my last day in an advanced state of inebriation—eight years to the day after Jimi Hendrix passed away while in a similar state. One of us died that day. One of us got to live to see September 19. The adage couldn't be truer: Every alcoholic has their last drunk. It's just that some of us live to talk about it.

I realize that I have fewer days ahead of me now than behind me. I also know that some of the best moments of my life haven't happened yet, and I plan on enjoying the heck out of them when they arrive. I am unable to buy an extended warranty for my sobriety so expect to see me here into the foreseeable future.

I know 43 years sounds impressive. And you should darn well be impressed. But not with me. With God. Make no mistake. It was his idea for me to get sober, not mine.

J.W.
Johnston, Iowa

Heaven on Earth

April 2024

I have gone to many meetings and AA functions over the years. And I have had many AA commitments. They have all been a blessing, especially when they involve Twelfth Step work.

In fact, I've only been to one bad meeting and it's the one that sporadically jumps up between my ears. It's a part of me. Negative thoughts stick in my head like flies on flypaper. I can't seem to shake myself free of these thoughts. It's all me, and that's when the bad meeting begins.

Of all the other things I've done to get the message in AA, I've fortunately listened to a few good spiritual advisors. One is my sponsor. He suggested that these bad meetings in my head needed a secretary. He volunteered me to be my own secretary when I can't sleep or think straight. My job is to grab a pencil or the keyboard of my computer and record every thought I'm having and what I think everyone is saying about me.

Two things immediately happen when I take up the secretary's position. I find out stuff about myself that I need to work on, which eventually helps me have a better day or night. And listening to the negative committee gets boring, and that makes me fall asleep. It's a neat trick. Thanks, sponsor, for the suggestion! This activity also alleviates the pain of me being me. Sometimes I'm too tired to keep up with the meeting in my head, so I go to sleep instead. It's a solid cure to my nights of insomnia.

Over the last 39 years and growing, I've learned that this program is not all about me. It's about one drunk talking to another. However, I'm 72 years young and growing older in a trailer park way out in the country. I enjoy it out here. It's a bird flyway, full of beautiful fishing spots and water sports. There are a few practicing alcoholics who live around here, but those belonging to our Fellowship seem rare. I cannot get out to do as many hospitals and institutions meetings as I would like.

There are very few AA meetings where I live. All of them are at least 10 miles away on the other side of the river over a drawbridge. Sometimes the bridge is up for a long time and the meeting may be half over when I finally get there.

Often my daily meetings are with my Grapevine. Even the phone and virtual meetings are challenging because of the many hang-ups, disconnects and other communication problems I have out here. I could easily be frustrated and consumed with negative thoughts, but this is good spot for the secretary to get busy writing things down. I pray to the God of my understanding instead. And that works perfectly. How cool is that?

As I trudge my road of happy destiny, looking at my rearview of AA in my past, I reflect on the saying "this too shall pass." I also see new friends coming my way often. They live in other parts of the Sacramento Delta, less than 10 miles away. There are a few oldtimers with oodles more years than my mere 39.

I have found a place to retire in peace. It's my heaven on earth here. I have sobriety, a wife, a dog, a garden and a studio-woodshop for art. I'm a dad and a grandparent—everything I could want as a sober member of AA. And it's all a grand gift from God.

Today God's love is immense, even more than I could write about here. I may be led this way in solitude, but I'm definitely not alone. But do you know what could mess this wonderful life up in a "sip-second"? Right! You know. Let's not go there.

Dea R-G.
Isleton, California

More Than Enough

January 2020

This morning I was awakened by a dream of embarrassment and fear, and it got me to thinking about self-respect and faith, as well as their opposites, and what life in the Twelve Steps has meant for me.

Before AA I had very little personal promise or much hope of ever changing what I thought was an ongoing spiral into what I called "badland." I was convinced that I was inherently worthless. I had so often disappointed my loved ones and myself that I felt I wasn't really worth having any kind of a loving God. Now I know that isn't true.

Eventually through the program, I was able to rise and shine and get ahold of my self-respect. I can now be grateful to a loving God that what I had was just a bad dream left over from my old life. He thankfully has replaced that with a new vision. It's nice to hold your head up after you haven't for a long time.

Today little things are such a blessing: Throwing on fresh clothes, walking out my door, saying a quick hi to the neighbors, enjoying a cup of coffee. Just appreciating the outdoors and fresh air is really more than enough.

The relief of not having to reach for a drink to keep the bogeyman away, letting go of the need to be powerful to cover up all my insecurities—it's all priceless. That old way of doing things is finally over. I am so thankful that the God of my understanding has the ball now. My job is to try not to take it back.

Judy H.
Claremont, California

Sweeter and Sweeter

March 2017

I started drinking whiskey at age 15. Was it fun? I would pass out, have bed spins, get sick, not remember how or when I got home, what I did or whom I was with.

Then I switched to beer. Was it fun? I was broke, unable to sleep without a buzz and I never felt rested. I made many hospital visits and had high blood pressure and mini strokes. I didn't care about anyone or anything except beer. I also had two DUIs, a divorce, and even wrecked into a tree.

Fun? Every day I thank God for my sobriety and those who helped make me whole again. Life is so much better and sweeter now. I wish I had known that at age 15, instead of 51. I do, however, intend to enjoy the rest of my life in blissful sobriety. Now that's what I call fun.

Glenn F.
Largo, Florida

A Place in the Sun

February 2016

In the course of my alcoholism, I spent years in therapy and hundreds of thousands of dollars on doctor visits and medications. I suffered an intense suicidal depression and was labeled bipolar.

The April before coming into AA, I planned to kill myself. One day after work, I went home to end my life. I had been planning to do it for years, considering various options and performing research on the best means of doing so. So when I went to bed that April night, I waited for the house to settle down so that I could take a lethal dose of pills. I wasn't thinking about a thing—not my wife or my child. I just lay there and waited. After all those years of planning, my life was crumbling around me, and the final solution to all of it was tucked away next to me in a bedside drawer. Amazingly, I did not fill my drink and take the pills. Instead, I passed out. I awoke the next day with something I'd never had: a willingness to change.

The next eight months were tumultuous. First I lost my job; then the state got involved in my life. I was forced to quit drinking. I was dry now, but not clean and sober. A funny thing happened on my way to sobriety however. Even with an active pill addiction, without alcohol my life started to change. Suddenly, my doctors didn't think I was bipolar. Over time, they took me off my last medication and I came into AA. I started a new job and life got better for my family.

One month into sobriety, while working Step Two with my sponsor, I took my family to San Diego for a vacation. The fact that I was alive to be there and had a job to pay for it was amazing. One afternoon, we went to a dolphin show. It was one of those beautiful San Diego days; the sun was shining and the air warm. We sat down in the grandstands and got ready for the show. Out came the dolphins and the performers, all set to music. The show was nice, but I saw very little of it. My eyes and my heart were watching my 2-year-old daughter.

She was so excited as she watched the show. Her face lit up with such intense joy; I'd never seen so much happiness on another person's face. I was enjoying the show through my daughter's eyes, when I was suddenly filled with intense gratitude and light for being alive to witness the moment. For the first time, I paused to ask myself, Why? Why was I alive in this moment?

I had come into the Fellowship of AA an atheist. I used to call myself an agnostic, because I always felt it was disrespectful to openly deny the existence of someone else's God. During my first month in AA, I stared at those Steps on the wall with great fear, wondering how I could ever get past the need to believe in a God of my understanding.

I thought about how my life had changed since that April night I was going to kill myself. I had stability at home now; I was free from suicidal depression and psychiatric medication, with the beginnings of real happiness I'd not known for 10 years. Why hadn't I done the easy thing that dark night and simply filled that glass and taken the pills? Even in my alcoholism, I was always a man of action. When I made plans, I acted on them. It was such a mystery that I hadn't taken those pills that night. But right there, on a sunny afternoon, while sitting in the stands with my daughter, I realized that such things do not happen by accident. The thought shook me to the core: A power greater than myself had reached into my life that lonely April night.

Tears began to stream down my face. For the first time in my life, I felt the presence of God. While working Step Two with my sponsor, I had wondered how I could ever come to believe a power greater than myself could restore me to sanity. I now realized he already had.

It turns out I found a God of my understanding through the light and eyes of my daughter.

Kevin F.
Vancouver, Washington

CHAPTER EIGHT

Living Life to Its Fullest

Enjoying sobriety, getting back into the world, making your dreams come true

What do AA members consider a rich, full life? It depends on the person of course, but a key ingredient is gratitude. We are thankful that we are no longer drunk and have a chance to go out and enjoy life and fulfill early promises we made to ourselves. This chapter is full of wonderful examples.

In the story "Dreams Come True," Snow P. recalls how she believed alcohol fueled her dreams, when in fact it killed them. She had so many chances that disintegrated into wild parties and hangovers. But one day she had enough and came to AA. "I have been able to accomplish every new dream that was born in my heart," she writes. "I did get a college education, marry a wonderful man and have three children. I now have six grandchildren. I have traveled all over the world and only just returned from riding a camel at the Giza pyramids in Egypt."

In "Joy on a Full Moon," Paul L. writes, "One of the many blessings of recovery is that I now go on many of the adventures I used to only talk about while drinking at the bar." One such adventure was biking up a beautiful mountain road in Glacier National Park at night to watch a full moon, joined by members of his home group—"a rolling AA meeting," as he puts it. Repeated year after year, this ride reminds him that being sober means to give thanks for what you have.

Dreams Come True

September 2025

When I was in high school, one of my fellow students loved to dance and wound up getting onto a popular TV dance show. I could not imagine how she accomplished that. To me that seemed as foreign as going to the moon.

Anything I could think of doing with my limited skills, experience and capabilities had no chance of developing into something real or even becoming a dream. Alcohol thwarted me at every turn. I would come up with a good idea and then drink to improve it, but what I did by drinking was kill it. I would encounter people who believed in me and wanted to help me, but I didn't know why or what I could do with their help.

One woman once let me use the back room of her real estate office as a painting studio. She thought I was really talented for a self-taught artist. I painted like crazy; then she retired and gave me the whole building to create something with. After I tiled the floors by hand, painted the outside of the building and got more artists to consign paintings, I had a great opening-night party. But I had no business experience, no art degree and no mentor to guide me. I just lived in the back of the gallery in a little room for two years, drinking while I gradually lost everything. I only opened the store on weekends so my wild parties could continue. I didn't have to worry about driving, and that nice woman only charged me $28 a month in rent.

I eventually knew I had to change something, but it never occurred to me to change myself. I tried to go to art school, but I dropped out after three weeks and went straight to a bar at 10:30 in the morning in downtown Manhattan. I knew I could not sustain any plan, as everything was so overwhelming. I had no one to walk me through the process of growing up and all I could do was turn to alcohol for help.

As they say, I took a drink, then the drink took a drink, then the drink took me. An education was not a possibility for me then.

I had already been married as a teenager to another alcoholic and that was "a bad movie" as they say, and I was happy to be out of it. Dreams of becoming a mother? Not a possibility with one sick relationship after another. Dreams of travel? I wondered what the kids on the Jersey Shore were doing, but had no idea how to get there. I just kept stumbling through my life, letting the drink decide my next move.

When I got a job as a receptionist and everyone in the office drank like I did, it was a win. They gave me promotion after promotion so someone could get the work done. I made enough money to take out a bank loan to buy furniture. My clothes and what I drank changed, but nothing else. After a night of drinking martinis, I would wake up with the hangover from hell, the same as I did with tequila. I would swear I was never doing that again, and by that night, there I was on the barstool again. I had an apartment, a car and a career, but the inside of me was deteriorating as if I were drinking battery acid. The very bottom came finally in my kitchen, where God was waiting for me.

That day in my kitchen was many moons ago. Through the grace and mercy of God and the people I found in AA, I've been able to accomplish sobriety every single day since by following the simple directions. As a benefit of sober life, I have been able to accomplish every new dream that was born in my heart. I did get a college education, marry a wonderful man and have three children. I now have six grandchildren. I have traveled all over the world and just returned from riding a camel at the Giza pyramids in Egypt.

I could have never even dreamed my life would be like this when I was drinking, but God and the good people of AA helped me to grow up and claim the magic. I can never repay all the gifts I've been given, so I keep writing. Please stay hopeful, as God will meet you anywhere!

Snow P.
Boca Raton, Florida

Friends in Every Port

August 2023

By the grace of God, I was sober for 21 years in the Navy until I retired from service. It was a career I would have never had without AA. One of the blessings I received was attending AA meetings all over the world. But there's one experience that has stuck with me over the years.

We were anchored in Hong Kong harbor. It was an early morning, and I was irritated for no good reason. I was tired, but we sailors are always tired. The city smelled bad, and there were too many people around. It was humid, the sun was too bright and my feet hurt. I was starting to feel sorry for myself. A lot of bad thoughts were going on between my ears.

But I had a goal. There was a 1 P.M. AA meeting up the hill from the ship. When I got there, I was sweating and miserable, with the mess and not a message. There were about eight members in the meeting room. I really don't remember much except that I was disappointed that they had instant coffee. One guy chatted with me outside about the upcoming turnover of Hong Kong to mainland China. A woman told me about another AA meeting. I traded an American cigarette for a British one with a young man. Soon I started to feel like I belonged to these alcoholics. They all went off to their jobs and I was alone again on the sidewalk—but now I wasn't lonely anymore. My thinking was different; the world felt different. Instead of the city, I smelled flowers. I was able to accept the humidity. Even the people seemed different. They seemed excited, people from all around the world, all God's children. I got excited to take the train up to Victoria's Peak and see the view. It was a spiritual experience.

I know that God is in our AA meeting room, but is that enough? Can I join in God's world only in a room of drunks? The people in the streets of Hong Kong didn't change, the weather didn't change—I did. I allowed myself to be in God's world. I saw that I needed something bigger beyond that group. God was not only in our AA room, but also in those strangers outside of the rooms. It was time for me to stop limiting God. I used to live in the world and visit AA—now I live in AA and visit the world.

Back then I had many more years of travel ahead of me. When I was sent to locations where there weren't any AA meetings, I learned to connect with people in other spiritual beliefs. I needed to find God wherever I was. I now have 34 years of sobriety and I don't travel much anymore since I've retired from the Navy. I've had the same home group since 2014. It's been a big adjustment learning to live in one place. Occasionally I'll get an itch to move somewhere different, but that feeling passes. However, if I should move, I know there will be an AA meeting there. And if not, God will be.

Russell T.
Bellevue, Washington

Hitting the Road
May 2025

My wife Pat and I just returned home from a fabulous vacation where we got to cross two more items off our bucket list. We both love to travel, and the gift of sobriety has enabled us to wander.

I got sober in July of 1983 after personally acquainting myself with "pitiful and incomprehensible demoralization." I thought for sure my life was over after I joined AA because I was never going to be able to drink again. No more fun. I was certain I would never again be able to dance to live music, snow ski, water ski, golf or fish, as all these activities required massive quantities of beer (and other things).

I also loved to travel and used to spend long weekends once or twice a year in the Rocky Mountains. I can't tell you how overjoyed I was when my first sponsor explained to me that yes, I could still do all these things and more without drinking. I learned I could even attend what the Big Book calls "plain ordinary whoopee parties," as well as Grateful Dead concerts! My sponsor even took me to my first sober concert. We had a blast dancing for three hours to Jerry and the rest of the Grateful Dead at the Red Rocks in Colorado.

In sobriety I became a certified scuba diver and traveled to 13 countries and logged more than 400 dives. When I was drinking, a big trip for me was a weekend in the mountains. Now a big trip is being gone more than a month or crossing the International Date Line.

My wife and I have been so blessed to attend AA meetings not only all over Nebraska, but across the United States and the world. Whenever and wherever Pat and I travel we always check to see where the AA meetings are and make plans to attend. Once after a meeting on the Caribbean island St. Lucia, some of the locals asked us to come to their house the next day (Christmas) to help celebrate their sponsor's 25th sober anniversary. What a treat! It's my belief that I have over two million friends in this wonderful Fellowship, but most of them I just haven't met yet.

So this brings me to last week. Pat and I were visiting New York City for the first time. Stepping Stones, the historic home of Lois and Bill in Bedford Hills, New York, has been on our bucket list for many years. And ever since I learned that you could visit our General Service Office (GSO) and see the Archives, we've wanted to check it out too. We got to go to Founders' Day in Akron, Ohio many years ago and it was indeed a spiritual experience. For this small-town Nebraska boy however, going to New York City to see GSO and the Archives department and then getting to attend the Friday morning AA meeting held there, I was literally overcome. What a wonderful feeling it was of being "home no matter where I am" when a member of the staff asked me to give the lead share for the meeting. What a day!

I want to thank everyone in attendance that Friday—I can't name names but you all know who you are. Pat and I are forever in awe of your service and dedication to our beloved Fellowship. May God bless all of you at our GSO. Thanks for saving my life today—and every day.

Dave H.
Lincoln, Nebraska

Be Anything, Go Anywhere

August 2023

Sobriety has given me so much more freedom to experience the world. I'm not afraid to travel to far-off lands, including travel by sea.

A while ago, I had the opportunity to scuba dive in the Far East. I was not familiar with the dive party I was with, but I had my Higher Power with me. The conditions were perfect. There were blue skies, smooth water, low current and warm sun. Once in the water, we immediately descended to 65 feet. The calmness took over when everyone buddied up and we began exploring.

My experience with meditation and breathing helped me relax and enjoy the ride. A new freedom set in, and I felt connected with my creator. The weightlessness of being underwater is a wonderful gift. The sheer lightness of moving under the sea is truly magical and freeing.

Remembering how I felt when I was newly sober always comes to mind in such situations. Being in touch with my body and breathing is magnified by my awareness of how small I am in the vastness of the universe. Sobriety and the power of AA has taught me I can be anything and go anywhere.

My spiritual growth expands when I continue showing up and when I'm willing to do what might feel uncomfortable to me at first, but which most always becomes a blessing. Thank you AA and Grapevine, for keeping me sober and sharing all the many gifts life has to offer as I continue on this spiritual path.

Cathy P.
Novato, California

Joy on a Full Moon

November 2024

One of the many blessings of recovery is that I now go on many of the adventures I used to only talk about while drinking at the bar.

Glacier National Park is a short 45 minutes from the town where I live. Riding my bicycle up Going-to-the-Sun Road during a full moon was one of the adventures I had always dreamed about. After I got sober and worked the Steps with my sponsor, I began to get my life back and decided to go on this biking adventure. I started taking short local rides before AA meetings to get myself in shape and familiarize myself with my bicycle.

I told members in my home group about my idea and some of them were interested in participating in the ride. We started meeting weekly for a 90-minute, no-drop ride around town and the surrounding countryside. On a no-drop ride everyone works together to make sure even the slowest rider is supported on the ride.

I was amazed at what I learned from other members while riding together. Some had grown up in this town and had great stories to tell. Everyone had spent some time on a bicycle and we each shared the adventures of our first rides with one another.

We finally picked a date on a full moon. We made arrangements for carpooling and set out on our ride. Eight people showed up. We also had three people show up who didn't want to ride but were willing to drive a "sag wagon" behind us to pick up stragglers.

Our adventure began at the Loop on Going-to-the-Sun Road to Logan Pass at 7 in the evening, just in time to be awed by the alpenglow of a setting sun on the Garden Wall. The eight-mile ride took about two hours, and it was like a rolling AA meeting. Some of the more experienced riders were faster and did their visiting after they reached the pass.

Others of us happily chatted as we pedaled our way to the top. Along the way, we got words of encouragement from the drivers of the sag wagons.

At the top of the pass we were treated to a spectacular moonrise over Mount Heavy Runner just as the sun set behind the Livingston range. The drivers of the sag wagons met us at the pass with warm clothes, lights for the ride down, coffee, cocoa and other treats, while we had an impromptu gratitude meeting in the parking lot. At around 10 in the evening, we strapped on our bike lights and coasted down to the Loop in the glow of the full moon. What had taken us two hours to ride up took 20 minutes to ride down. What a joy. I began to understand fully what the fellowship of AA means.

Since that first ride a dozen years ago, our Full Moon ride up Going-to-the-Sun Road has become an annual event. We have had as few as two riders and as many as 15. We have even had visiting tourists ride up with us. Many non-bike riders drive the sag wagons and experience the beauty of the park and the camaraderie of the fellowship. I get to learn so much about sobriety and life from my fellow riders.

This past year, I experienced some of the road bumps that occur on our journey through life. After 36 years of marriage, my wife wanted a divorce, and I became consumed with trying to get my life back on track. I decided to blow off the annual bike ride to focus on what I thought needed to be done. I was overwhelmed with inquiries about when we were going to do the ride, but I said I was too busy and couldn't do it. Another member of our group knew the importance of this event to our members and picked up the mantle of organizer. The ride was set.

I still didn't plan on participating, but at the last minute everything came together, and I was able to join them. It turned out to be the best ride ever (although I say that every year). That ride turned out to be loaded with poignant lessons for me. I felt such a rush getting to the starting point, even though I worried that I wasn't in good enough condition to accomplish the ride. I rode in the back of the group and got to visit with some of the riders I don't see very often. I rode slower than usual, and it was cool that evening, so about five miles up I stopped to put on my windbreaker.

As I looked around before getting back on my bicycle, I noticed my car keys on the ground between my shoes. In the process of pulling my jacket out of my jersey pocket, I had unknowingly dropped the keys. I started to berate myself. I have always been harder on myself than anyone else could ever be. My next thought was, Wait, stop that, give thanks that you noticed them at dusk rather than having to look for them when you got back to your car when it would be dark, and you would have no idea where you had lost them. I immediately realized how fortunate I had been in finding the keys and gave thanks for that.

A little farther on, I was resting along the side of the road when several elite riders came by. They stopped and we enjoyed the gloaming of the evening stretching out along Lake McDonald far below. As we chatted about our experiences on this road, they asked if I had any other warmer clothes and I said yes, I had some arm warmers. They were surprised I had nothing for my legs, but I assured them I would be fine. They rode on, and after waiting for the final two riders in our group, I continued up the road as well.

As I pedaled around Oberlin Bend before the final stretch to the pass, most of our group went zipping on down the road in the opposite direction. They had gotten cold and decided it was time to descend. When I got to the top, I had the whole place to myself, not another vehicle or rider in sight. It was cold so I went through my pockets to pull out my warmer clothes. The first thing I pulled out was a single leg warmer. It turned out that was the only warm article of clothing I had on me. The other clothes I brought were carried by the other riders in our group who had already gone on down the road. I was at least able to give thanks for what I had, rather than beat myself up.

Because of the cold (and lack of warm clothes), I decided I better leave. I would check with the final two riders on my way down. I strapped on my bike light and headed down the winding road. I made it about 100 yards before the light blinked off. I pulled over to the side of the road in the glow of the moon and tried to troubleshoot the light. There was no fixing it and my extra light was with the riders who had already descended. I thought, No problem. There was a full moon and I felt I had enough light to make it the remaining miles down to the cars. I didn't consider the moon shadow created by the cliffs along the road and when I rode into the shadows the world turned pitch black. I made it about 50 feet in the darkness before I realized this was really dangerous.

As I looked down the road stretching below me, I saw the dim blinking lights from our final two riders. I waited for them and when they made their way up to me, I asked for help. I asked them if they had an extra light. They had an extra pen light, so I turned around and followed them back up to the top of the pass.

The final ride down was not what I expected. It was colder, the ride was slower with the dimmer light and I was riding by myself. I was able to use that time to be grateful for the three lessons I had been given that day: Don't beat yourself up, give thanks for what you have, and it is OK to ask for help.

Thank you God.

Paul L.
Whitefish, Montana

Off to the Races

March 2017

My father started racing stock cars at a dirt track on the south side of Baltimore when I was just 3 years old. I immediately fell in love with the sport. Dad started out in the hobby division, which meant racing old jalopies with roll bars. Watching him race was a thrill even though his car was not nearly as fast as the top-division cars driven by the likes of Frankie Schneider and Johnny Roberts.

We moved out to western Maryland a few years later. Dad kept racing. He had moved up to the sportsman division and raced at several tracks in northern Virginia and West Virginia. I learned in school that other families went camping or fishing and stuff like that. We hooked up that racecar and headed to as many as three different tracks in one weekend. The season lasted from April until October. I spent the winters watching Dad and his friends work on their cars.

Racing is very expensive. After a few more years, my father had to give up driving stock cars. He said he caught himself spending grocery money on carburetors one time too many. Even though he hadn't raced in NASCAR's elite Grand National division, we followed them very closely and continued to do so after my father quit racing.

My favorite driver was Fireball Roberts. Dad was a Joe Weatherly fan. Mom rooted first for Lee Petty and later for his son, Richard. Stock car racing wasn't popular in the Northeast. I often had to explain that being a race fan didn't mean I was necessarily into Indianapolis-type cars or sports cars. We were living in Delaware when the racing community lost both Fireball and Joe in crashes. Most of my school chums had no clue why I was so upset.

When I was in high school, we moved to the Philadelphia area. Dad was into drag racing then. He had a car he ran every Sunday. Once I got my license, I tried my hand at it too, but not with a lot of success. We still had friends who raced stock cars at the local short tracks. I went with them when I could. I continued to closely follow NASCAR.

After I graduated from high school, I attended college at a small upstate school close to the New York border. It was there that I picked up my first drink. The drinking age in New York was 18 then. I was legal. I loved the effect, but for the most part drinking was a weekend activity. During the week I stayed sober and studied. There were a few times when I was too drunk to drive but drove anyway. I was clearly in denial of my problem.

After college, I secured a teaching position near Philadelphia. My alcoholic progression was slow but steady. I never drank in the mornings or at work. But by my mid-20s, I was drinking every evening, either at home or in bars. By my mid-30s, I found myself checking into a rehab.

I'll never forget the feeling of freedom from the bondage of alcoholism I felt when I drove away from that facility. Before I went in, I couldn't even go one day without a drink. Now the compulsion was lifted. I managed to get almost two years sober with occasional AA meeting attendance.

Eventually, however, that old denial kicked back in. Maybe I wasn't a real alcoholic after all. Maybe if I tried again I would be able to drink successfully. That stinking thinking cost me another six years of hanging out in bars every night.

At age 43, I was arrested for driving under the influence. That got me back into the rooms of AA. After about a week of sobriety, I got back that feeling of freedom I had experienced eight years before. I decided then that there was no way I was going to let it go again. I began to attend AA meetings daily and started to work the program.

By this time, NASCAR had been racing for several years at Pocono Raceway in Pennsylvania and Dover Raceway in Delaware. I had attended most of these races and consumed a lot of alcohol while I was there. My new sobriety left me with a dilemma. Did I have to give up this sport that I loved because of the danger of people, places and things? Or could I go anywhere I wanted so long as I had a good reason for being there and was on strong spiritual ground, as it says in the Big Book?

After nine months of sobriety, I attended a NASCAR race in Dover. I took another AA member with me who had more than 20 years of sobriety. Later that summer I purchased a used trailer that I towed to the race in the Poconos. From there, I went to races in Indianapolis, Michigan, Tennessee and South Carolina. I picked up my one-year chip at a meeting in Florence, not far from the Darlington Raceway. I found the key to staying sober was regular attendance at meetings in these race towns just as attending meetings at home.

I have no doubt that the ability to complete my teaching career was due to my sobriety. I retired at 55 and bought a new motor home. Today, after more than 20 years of sobriety, I go to at least a dozen races a year. Not only do I get to enjoy the racing, but I also love the fellowship I have found in the rooms. It is so cool to walk into that

AA group in Harrisburg, North Carolina, near the Charlotte Motor Speedway, and hear those boys say, "Here comes Ted. The race must be back in town!" The same thing happens in Bristol, Richmond, Dover, Pocono, Homestead and lots of other race towns. I'm so grateful to my friends in these rooms because they keep me sober so I can enjoy the racing that I love.

If you attend a NASCAR race, look for me. I'll be in the RV with the "Easy Does It" sticker in the windshield.

Ted C.
Newton, Pennsylvania

The Rowdiest, Rockingest Group

March 2017

When people think about fun in sobriety, their thoughts often go to sober bowling, hanging out at the local diner, drinking bad coffee or dancing the night away at a fellowship dance. For me, the most fun I have in sobriety is right here at my Saturday night meeting, surrounded by old friends and experiencing the joy of welcoming a newcomer. What could be more fun?

I never danced on tables or trashed hotel rooms. I was a "sofa drunk." I never came to in a strange country surrounded by empty bottles of tequila. I never stole a car, a tractor, a snowmobile or a farm animal while in a blackout. And I never drank anybody under a table.

I was the mom who drank. I was the wife and teacher who drank. And I did it very quietly. Every day and every night I drank, and those days and nights stretched into years—years when my children grew up and my marriage grew strained and my career stagnated—all unnoticed by me.

Back then, my idea of fun was drawing the blinds and getting into bed with a tumblerful of wine and an old paperback.

When I hear people talk about all the crazy adventures they had while drinking, I can't really relate. Aside from a few moments in college (I vaguely remember singing Patsy Cline on the hood of a car) drinking wasn't linked to fun. Alcohol was soothing. It allowed me to handle the stress and anxiety of being a mom and working fulltime as a middle-school teacher.

Most of all, alcohol provided me with obliteration. The traumas of my childhood were forgotten the moment I had that first sip of chardonnay. It shut down the incessant chatter in my head and let me feel some peace.

So I never expected AA would be fun. How could it be? I figured the Fellowship would be filled with grumpy old men with coffee-stained teeth and their sullen, disappointed wives. I didn't have any fun while I was drinking and I resigned myself to the fact that I wouldn't have fun in sobriety either.

It may come as a bit of a shock then, that I managed to pick the rowdiest, wildest, rockingest home group in the entire state of Maine: The Old Orchard Beach Beginners' Meeting—known to everyone from around these parts as "The Greatest Group in the Galaxy." It sometimes feels more like a big family reunion than an AA meeting, especially in the summer when all our friends "from away" come in.

When I first walked into our meeting hall back in 2009, I was struck by the wall of sound. It wasn't just laughter, but guffawing, knee-slapping laughter, the kind you can't help but laugh along with. Believe me, it had been a long time since I'd found a reason to laugh. I certainly didn't expect to find laughter in the dingy basement of a Methodist church.

The next thing that happened was the warm greeting I got, yelled at top volume along with a vigorous handshake and smile. "Welcome," my new friends said. "You're in the right place."

That first AA meeting is a bit of a blur now. What I remember most is the energy of the pre-meeting, the coming together of such disparate fellows to celebrate life. I remember too the shock of the first clap of the gavel, followed by instantaneous silence and the sweet sound of the Serenity Prayer. Even today, that sudden shift from cacophony to calm fills me with gratitude for the special place I call my home group.

As it happens, sobriety has been a whole lot more fun than drinking was. My life has become so much richer and fuller in the six years since I got sober. I no longer crave obliteration. I've learned that being fully aware and connected to others is the key to enjoying life.

I've been to lots of sober parties and dances, mostly with women from my home group. I've gone to picnics and sober roundups. I've gone hiking and spent days at the beach with the new friends I've made in AA. And I've even been to a wedding in AA.

But honestly, the most fun of all is spending Saturday nights with the men and women from The Greatest Group in the Galaxy, the people who loved me and guided me in my early days, the people who continue to support me, challenge me, and help me live each day happy, joyous and free.

Gwyneth N.
Saco, Maine

CHAPTER NINE

The Gift of Gratitude

Taking time to remember that gratitude is always within reach

In the heartfelt and sometimes humorous stories in this chapter, AA members demonstrate that gratitude "goes hand in hand with serenity," as Jim W. writes in his story "Etched in Stone," adding, "The more things I find to be grateful for, the more my serenity increases."

Sometimes the message repeats every day of the year. Jayson K.'s wonderful yearlong gratitude list in the story "Another Beautiful Year" includes: "365 breakfasts where I can look at my family as a fully present husband and father."

Finding gratitude isn't always easy when you're having a really bad day Jim B. tells us in "One of Those Days." But then he literally steps into a puddle, looks down and finds a thin wall-hanging of the Serenity Prayer, complete with praying hands. "I laughed out loud, glanced upward, and said, 'Message received!'" he recalls.

Sometimes we're able to muster up gratitude in a unique and different way. In the story "Trying to Be Ungrateful," Mark K. decides to make an "ingratitude list." As it turns out, it's a short one, which makes his gratitude list so much longer and more important. "I actually have so many blessings I can't count them all," he realizes.

A Deep Breath

October 2024

Gratitude has been a foundation for my life since July of 1996. My gratitude began the second day I stayed sober for a 24-hour period. I remember it well because that was the 4th of July, a day I would be typically drowning in liquor.

The thing that helped me the most when my husband left me after 16 years of marriage was writing a gratitude list every night, which consisted of at least five things for which I could be grateful. Some days the list consisted of very simple things like, "Grateful this day has finally ended," and "Grateful I had enough to eat today," and "Grateful I got out of bed today." On other days, my list was full of amazing things like, "Grateful that I'm able to shovel the snow and enjoy the quiet hush that the blanket of snow on the ground provides," and "Grateful that I can travel to a foreign country by myself and not be afraid of asking for directions or help."

Staying in an attitude of gratitude is what has allowed me to finally come to a place of forgiveness toward my now-ex-husband. I realized that in order to stay in a place of gratitude, I had to let go of that burdensome resentment and anger. It weighed me down spiritually and emotionally. I realized that gratitude and anger could not coexist in my soul. If I was vigilant in searching daily for things to be grateful for, I did not have much time left over to go to that place of anger and resentment. I just could not stay grateful and be angry at the same time.

Most of the time now gratitude wins hands down. Staying angry or resentful just takes too much out of me, while it takes very little energy to remain grateful. I find that I can be grateful and still have plenty of energy left over for participating in my life and all the things it has to offer.

Gratitude is a state of mind, an emotion, an attitude, a condition of the soul, a prayer (if you will). I find that after writing in my gratitude journal, I feel as if I've just taken a very deep breath and released it ever so slowly. A feeling of peace always comes over me while I'm journaling. I've found that no matter what life has to offer, if I stay in an attitude of gratitude, I can pretty much deal with anything.

Stefania R.
Pingree Grove, Illinois

Another Beautiful Year

January 2025

A New Year's gratitude list for the next 365—one day at a time:

365 promises I will make to myself that I will not drink for 24 hours.

365 mornings where I get to awaken to a clear head with full retention of the previous day's events.

365 breakfasts where I can look at my family as a fully present husband and father.

365 days knowing I'm not alone nor the first to have sought help for my alcoholism.

365 days of lies I won't have to tell or stories to get straight in order to hide my drinking.

365 opportunities to learn from my disease and help others see it doesn't define who we are.

365 promises I get to keep, as today is just the beginning.

Jayson K.
Champlin, Minnesota

One of Those Days

February 2024

When I was sober for a fairly short time in AA and in a generally receptive attitude about some of the basics I was hearing at meetings, I had an incident that has never left my memory since.

It was one of those February mornings when everything seemed to be going wrong, starting with stepping on the dog's tail as I came down the stairs, launching him into a howling fury that pierced the serenity of the morning for the rest of the household, followed by discovering that the milk I poured on my cereal was sour. After that, I was unable to find the gloves I needed in order to shovel a path to the garage.

The slippery 20-mile trip into the city was nerve-wracking, but I made it to the parking lot and immediately closed the corner of my good topcoat in the car door. Fumbling for my keys, I managed to extricate my coat, but the streak of grease it had acquired in that brief moment seemed to be saying, "This is how your whole day is going to go."

I had also neglected to bring the proper parking fee, but the attendant agreed to let me ride until the next day and I thought to myself, What else can go wrong?

I shouldn't have asked.

As I was leaving the lot, my foot broke through a thin layer of ice in a pothole and the resulting "hot foot" did nothing to help my attitude. And yet I felt something at the bottom of the frosty mud puddle, and reaching down I picked out a flat gift box from one of the area's upscale stores. It appeared intact, so I opened it. Inside the box was a thin wall-hanging of the Serenity Prayer, complete with praying hands. I laughed out loud, glanced upward, and said, "Message received!"

The rest of the day, as I recall, went quite well.

It has been 40 years since that day, but it still serves as a reminder that sometimes I can literally trip over the obvious and, as long as I stay in tune with some of our program's "basics," things have a way of working out.

Jim B.
Macedon, New York

The Gift of Gratitude

November 2024

My daughter called me one day to ask the age-old question, "Is this all there is?" She was 28 years old and married to her handsome prince. She and her husband were both working in great jobs, living in Los Angeles in a funky bungalow with their two dogs. To all appearances they were living the dream.

"I get up in the morning, work all day, make dinner, watch TV, go to bed and do it all again the next day," she said. "Is this what the rest of my life is going to be like?"

I wanted to laugh and say, "For the next 30 years or so, yes!" My daughter had done everything right, got her degree, got married, got the good job, but somehow, now that she was "there," it just wasn't what she thought it was going to be.

I thought about how similar my life in sobriety has been to her life. When I was a newcomer in AA, I couldn't wait to get that 30-day chip. Then I wondered how I would ever make it to 90 days. Picking up that chip seemed like a huge achievement, and then came chips at six months and nine months, and that whole time I was dreaming of my bronze one-year medallion. Now that would be an achievement, I told myself.

But once I held each of those chips in my hand, I realized that my life was not really where I thought it should be. My marriage was hanging by a thread, my finances were a disaster, I was spread so thin you could see through me. I was trying to work full-time, going back to school, going to AA meetings every day, trying to be a good wife and reconnect with family. It all seemed like such a struggle, even a year into the program, after doing everything I was supposed to do: staying sober, getting a sponsor and working the Steps. Shouldn't my life have been transformed?

It seems like this happened again and again—at five years, at 10 years, at 20 years. Upon reaching each of these milestone anniversaries, I remember thinking, Now they will all listen to me and now I will be a sought-after speaker and now I will have a herd of sponsees quoting my wisdom.

And yet once someone handed me that medallion, my life was not transformed. I was still driving across town to get to the AA meeting early to make the coffee and open the doors and set up the laptop because nobody else seemed to be willing to help out. I was still doing the 16-week Step Study workshops every year, which usually started out with 20 women and lucky if five made it to Step Twelve.

Sponsees I had invested so much time and effort into either drifted away or drank. I wanted to yell to my Higher Power, "Is this all there is?" But what I secretly wanted to yell was, "What's in it for me? Where is my reward?" Sometimes I can be so blind. I imagine my Higher Power bopping her forehead in frustration and saying, "After all I've done for her!"

When I arrived in AA, I was working for minimum-wage pay as a receptionist, expecting my husband to ask for a divorce any day, deeply in debt, isolated and alone, with alcohol as my consoling companion. I was on the brink of disaster, and by simply crossing the threshold of an AA meeting, my life was transformed.

In AA, I found a new meaning to life, I found a God of my understanding. The universe that previously had seemed to have it out for me suddenly began showering me with random gifts and miracles that only I could see. I was given a program to follow, a fellowship of friends, the guidance of wise sponsors I could trust and call on at any time of day or night. It seemed that as long as I continued to go to meetings, stay sober, work these Steps and be of service there was no end to the magical life I began to lead.

There were ups and downs, deaths and divorce, but thanks to AA and a spiritual perspective, none of these things seemed unjust or tragic. This was the stuff of life, and because I was in AA, I had the tools not only to deal with life, but to see the good in all these challenges. It's like I was wearing spiritual armor. I found meaning in life and did not fear death. I should have died drunk or in jail. AA pulled me out of the trash, cleaned me up, injected me with sobriety, spirituality and sunshine and set me on my way.

So the next time my daughter asks me, "Is this all there is?" I can tell her that, at least from my own perspective, this life I have lived is a great and wonderful gift from the universe. Every dinner I get to make, every time I get to walk the dog, every meeting I get to attend—these are all part of the continuing stream of love that has been graced to me by God.

Deanna S.
Roswell, Georgia

Going in the Right Direction

September 2025

Our washing machine broke yesterday. My wife and I had to drive to the home improvement store, pick out a new machine, get it into the minivan, remove the old machine and install the new one. All this we did after work on Friday.

The task was made a little more difficult by the fact that we were going from side-by-side machines to a stackable configuration. That change involved the need to remove and modify the wire shelving and then figure out how to assemble the stackable kit.

Why am I sharing this? One of my most common comments to recovering alcoholics is that "Everything is easier sober."

And I lived that last night! Sober, it all got done. It wasn't the most exciting night I've ever had, but I went to sleep at 10:30 in the evening with two functioning laundry machines and a room ready to restock in the morning. But I do know how it could have gone down.

"Broken washer! Why me?" After two beers, then two more beers (after all, it had been a hard day), then one more for the road, I would have had my wife drive us to the store. I'd be overly chatty with the salesman and leave with whatever machines he wanted me to have after I showed him how smart I was. Then would come me struggling to get the machines into the van, then the fight to get the machines into the house. "Terrible design," I would say. "Missing directions, missing parts. They're so stupid!"

Then, bam, waking up the next morning feeling terrible with 15 empty beer cans nearby and wishing I didn't have to deal with the damn washing machine. I would then claim, "Some vandals must have come in last night and screwed with my tools. And look at this mess!"

I don't know if a drunk Matt would have ended up in the emergency room before the machine was even working, but I do know it would have been a three-day ordeal with a story we would remember (and mention) for years to come.

As it is, two weeks from now, if you ask my wife how the washing machine swap went, there's a good chance she'll hardly remember it—and I like it like that!

Everyone is better at everything when they're sober.

Matthew M.
Oak Park, Illinois

Etched in Stone

From: ***Dear Grapevine***
May 2024

One day when I was about six months sober, I was eating at a restaurant. At the checkout counter there was a box that had some polished stones with words etched on them. I browsed through the box, found one with the word "Gratitude" etched on it, and brought it home with me.

Over time, I would often misplace my stone. Whenever I would find it again, it would remind me to write a gratitude list. This last time I found it, I put it on my desk where I could see it every day. It now reminds me to make a gratitude list every morning.

For me, gratitude goes hand in hand with serenity. I cherish serenity most of all. The more things I find to be grateful for, the more my serenity increases. I'm grateful I've met so many wonderful people on this journey. I'm grateful I've repaired relationships that were falling apart during my drinking days. I'm grateful I get to help those who have come into AA after me. I'm grateful that my Higher Power has given me a new purpose in life.

Today, my usual response when asked how I'm doing is to say, "I'm alive, awake and sober—and if it gets any better, I don't know if I can handle it."

Jim W.
San Marcos, Texas

Trying to Be Ungrateful
March 2020

A while back, it seemed that at most of the AA meetings I attended, the topic turned out to be gratitude. Members shared about a variety of things they were grateful for, such as not having hangovers or waking up in jail. One solution that came up over and over again was to make a gratitude list to remind ourselves how thankful one can be.

One day after one of those meetings, I was having a cup of coffee with an AA friend. As we talked, my friend shared with me that he was in a serious funk, a funk so deep that even the gratitude list he made wasn't helping. It was at that point in our conversation that I had this intuitive thought. I figured that maybe he should try something different. I suggested that he make a list of all the things he was ungrateful for. Maybe that would help.

After I left, it occurred to me that I should practice what I had just preached. So I went home and made an "ingratitude list" myself. I must have been in denial or had a severe case of writer's block, because my ingratitude list was a short list. It consisted of problems of cleaning the swimming pool after a dust storm, driving in traffic and all of the people demanding my time. I discovered that all of my problems were "Cadillac problems"! And you know what? Because I made that ingratitude list, I rediscovered my gratitude list.

Doing this list reminded me to be grateful that I have nearly 30 years of continuous sobriety, with a nice life and a good marriage. I actually have so many blessings I can't count them all. It made me truly grateful for all the gifts I've received.

I'm here to tell you that gratitude sits at the top of my spiritual toolbox now. Gratitude has the utility of a Swiss Army knife; it can be used to fix most all my problems. Funny—it wasn't until I thought about what I was ungrateful for, that I realized how really good I have it.

I truly believe that saying we often hear in meetings: A grateful alcoholic is a sober alcoholic.

Mark K.

Casa Grande, Arizona

The Twelve Steps

1. We admitted we were powerless over alcohol—that our lives had become unmanageable.
2. Came to believe that a Power greater than ourselves could restore us to sanity.
3. Made a decision to turn our will and our lives over to the care of God *as we understood Him.*
4. Made a searching and fearless moral inventory of ourselves.
5. Admitted to God, to ourselves, and to another human being the exact nature of our wrongs.
6. Were entirely ready to have God remove all these defects of character.
7. Humbly asked Him to remove our shortcomings.
8. Made a list of all persons we had harmed, and became willing to make amends to them all.
9. Made direct amends to such people wherever possible, except when to do so would injure them or others.
10. Continued to take personal inventory and when we were wrong promptly admitted it.
11. Sought through prayer and meditation to improve our conscious contact with *God as we understood Him,* praying only for knowledge of His will for us and the power to carry that out.
12. Having had a spiritual awakening as the result of these steps, we tried to carry this message to alcoholics, and to practice these principles in all our affairs.

The Twelve Traditions

1. Our common welfare should come first; personal recovery depends upon A.A. unity.
2. For our group purpose there is but one ultimate authority—a loving God as He may express Himself in our group conscience. Our leaders are but trusted servants; they do not govern.
3. The only requirement for A.A. membership is a desire to stop drinking.
4. Each group should be autonomous except in matters affecting other groups or A.A. as a whole.
5. Each group has but one primary purpose—to carry its message to the alcoholic who still suffers.
6. An A.A. group ought never endorse, finance or lend the A.A. name to any related facility or outside enterprise, lest problems of money, property and prestige divert us from our primary purpose.
7. Every A.A. group ought to be fully self-supporting, declining outside contributions.
8. Alcoholics Anonymous should remain forever nonprofessional, but our service centers may employ special workers.
9. A.A., as such, ought never be organized; but we may create service boards or committees directly responsible to those they serve.
10. Alcoholics Anonymous has no opinion on outside issues; hence the A.A. name ought never be drawn into public controversy.
11. Our public relations policy is based on attraction rather than promotion; we need always maintain personal anonymity at the level of press, radio and films.
12. Anonymity is the spiritual foundation of all our traditions, ever reminding us to place principles before personalities.

AA Grapevine

AA Grapevine is AA's international monthly journal, published continuously since its first issue in June 1944. The AA pamphlet on AA Grapevine describes its scope and purpose this way: "As an integral part of Alcoholics Anonymous since 1944, the Grapevine publishes articles that reflect the full diversity of experience and thought found within the A.A. Fellowship, as does La Viña, the bimonthly Spanish-language magazine, first published in 1996. No one viewpoint or philosophy dominates their pages, and in determining content, the editorial staff relies on the principles of the Twelve Traditions."

In addition to magazines, AA Grapevine, Inc. also produces books, eBooks, audiobooks, mobile apps, a weekly podcast, an Instagram account, a YouTube channel and other items. It also offers a Grapevine Complete subscription, which includes the print magazine as well as complete online access, with new stories weekly, AudioGrapevine (the audio version of the magazine), the vast Grapevine Story Archive and current online issues of Grapevine and La Viña. For more information on AA Grapevine, or to subscribe to any of these, please visit the magazine's website at aagrapevine.org or write to:

AA Grapevine, Inc.
475 Riverside Drive
New York, NY 10115

Alcoholics Anonymous

AA's program of recovery is fully set forth in its basic text, *Alcoholics Anonymous* (commonly known as the Big Book), now in its Fourth Edition, as well as in *Twelve Steps and Twelve Traditions, Living Sober,* and other books. Information on AA can also be found on AA's website at www.aa.org, or by writing to:

Alcoholics Anonymous
Box 459
Grand Central Station
New York, NY 10163

For local resources, check your local telephone directory under "Alcoholics Anonymous." Four pamphlets, "This is A.A.," "Is A.A. For You?," "44 Questions," and "A Newcomer Asks" are also available from AA.